OREGON DESCENTS

A BACKCOUNTRY SKI GUIDE TO THE SOUTHERN CASCADES

David L. Waag

OREGON DESCENTS

Disclaimer

Backcountry skiing, snowboarding and mountaineering are inherently dangerous. People are injured and die participating in these activities. This book is no substitute for experience or skill and is not intended to teach you skills that will reduce the risks involved in mountain travel. This book is solely intended to direct you to a variety of ski mountaineering routes. It is in no way a substitute for education, experience and sound judgement.

Although every effort was made to present accurate data, errors may exist. The author assumes no responsibility for any problems that may arise from using this book.

© David L. Waag 1997
All Rights Reserved.

All photography, layout and design by the author unless otherwise indicated.
Overview map by Karen Holt

Printed in the USA using recycled paper and soy based inks.

ISBN: 0-9661746-0-7

Published by Free Heel Press, Portland, Oregon
PO Box 19556, Portland, OR 97280-0556
www.freeheelpress.com

Cover: Mt. Hood's Coe Glacier. May
Title page: Near the summit of Diamond Peak. March
Back cover: Skiing the Lunch Counter on Mt. Adams. November Photo: Roger Alfred

OREGON DESCENTS

Mt. Adams. July

ACKNOWLEDGMENTS

As with any large writing project, this book was completed with the help of others. With the inspiration, guidance, support and patience of many people, this book came to be. I would like to thank those people who actively participated, those with whom I have skied over the years and all those whose positive energy helped make *Oregon Descents* happen. The following people deserve a special thanks: Roger Alfred, David Evans, Rusty Harrison, Karen Holt, Matt Hutcheson, Wendy May, Tracy Schlapp and Jeff Schuh.

Finally, I need to thank my parents whose support and encouragement made this project a reality.

TABLE OF CONTENTS

FOREWORD — p. 10
PREFACE — p. 11
OVERVIEW MAP — p. 12

INTRODUCTION
  HOW TO USE THIS GUIDE — p. 13
  SEASONAL NOTES — p. 15
  BACKCOUNTRY ACCESS — p. 15
  CASCADE WEATHER AND SNOW — p. 18
  AVALANCHE AWARENESS — p. 23
  EQUIPMENT — p. 28

PART ONE - MT. HOOD — p. 30

MT. HOOD AREA
  TOM, DICK AND HARRY MT. — p. 32

SOUTH SIDE ROUTES — p. 36
  ALPINE TRAIL / GLADE TRAIL — p. 38
  CIRCUMNAVIGATION — p. 41
  CRATER ROCK — p. 45
  ILLUMINATION SADDLE — p. 48
  SUMMIT ROUTES — p. 51

EAST SIDE ROUTES — p. 55
- HEATHER CANYON — p. 57
- WHITE RIVER CANYON — p. 60
- WY'EAST — p. 63

NORTH SIDE ROUTES — p. 66
- BARRETT SPUR — p. 69
- COE GLACIER — p. 73
- COOPER SPUR — p. 76
- LADD GLACIER BOWLS — p. 81
- LANGILLE GLACIER BOWLS — p. 81
- SNOW DOME — p. 86

PART TWO - CENTRAL OREGON — p. 90

MT. JEFFERSON
- JEFFERSON PARK GLACIER — p. 91
- PARK BUTTE / PARK RIDGE — p. 95

THREE SISTERS WILDERNESS — p. 97

BROKEN TOP
- CRATER BOWL / SW RIDGE — p. 99

TABLE OF CONTENTS

MIDDLE SISTER
- SOUTHEAST RIDGE — p. 103
- PROUTY POINT SADDLE — p. 106

NORTH SISTER
- SOUTHEAST RIDGE — p. 108

SOUTH SISTER
- SOUTH SIDE — p. 110

DIAMOND PEAK
- WEST SIDE — p. 113

PART THREE - SOUTHERN OREGON — p. 117

MT. BAILEY
- EAST FACE / WEST FACE — p. 118

MT. McLOUGHLIN
- WEST SIDE — p. 122

MT. SHASTA (N. CALIFORNIA)
- WEST FACE — p. 126

PART FOUR - SOUTHERN WASHINGTON p. 131

GOAT ROCKS WILDERNESS
- SNOWGRASS FLATS — p. 133
- WHITE PASS — p. 136

MT. ADAMS
- SOUTH SIDE — p. 139
- CRESCENT GLACIER BOWLS — p. 142

MT. ST. HELENS
- PERMITS — p. 144
- CLIMBERS BIVY/MONITOR RIDGE — p. 146
- MARBLE MOUNTAIN / WORM FLOWS — p. 149
- BUTTE CAMP ROUTE — p. 152

APPENDIX
- AVALANCHE RESOURCES — p. 155
- WEATHER RESOURCES — p. 156
- RECOMMENDED READING — p. 157

INDEX p. 158

Kicking steps up Barrett Spur, Mt. Hood. June

FOREWORD

A guide to Oregon's backcountry? As if there are not enough folks out there already. It is not my wish or expectation that *Oregon Descents* will change the nature of skiing in Oregon. Rather, I hope this book will serve as a resource to the backcountry ski community, share new routes to explore and provide important information regarding access, terrain and potential hazards. We are drawn to the backcountry by our pursuit of solitude in the mountains and none of us wish to see our favorite local routes overrun or abused by new users. However, we all know the glory of a day in the mountains. It is for the good of the soul that we visit the backcountry and with respect for the mountain environment that we share our knowledge and continue to visit the mountains.

Cascade summer snowpack. August

PREFACE

Leaving a set of tracks in the snow has an unparalelled attraction. Whether you free your heel, lock your heel or board to make turns, tracks in snow are one the most ephemeral imprints we can make on this earth. Earning your turns is simply the most graceful way to leave such an imprint. Hike up, ski down. Why do we hike for hours only to descend in a fraction of the time? The answer lies within and, however you look at it, a day in the mountains is good for your soul. More and more people are discovering the appeal of backcountry skiing and ski mountaineering and this book is an effort to help you find your day in the mountains.

As a guide to alpine descents, the focus of this book is accessing terrain to ski or board down. Although all of the routes require an approach, *Oregon Descents* is not a touring guide. The routes described here require an intermediate to expert level of downhill technique and gear designed for downhill skiing or boarding. The Southern Cascade region offers relatively easy access. The mountains are not buried deep within a range but stand alone and offer short approaches as well as clean lines of descent. Although the majority of routes described in this book are best skied in spring, many are accessible in a variety of seasons and several are primarily winter routes.

Regardless of your method of travel, the time of year or your ability, the importance of safety cannot be over emphasized. Safe mountain travel requires knowledge of the area, map and compass skill, knowledge of the snowpack, understanding the weather and knowing your skiing or boarding limitations. *Oregon Descents* is a tool to help you access skiable terrain and help you plan and evaluate your Cascade skiing adventures.

OVERVIEW MAP

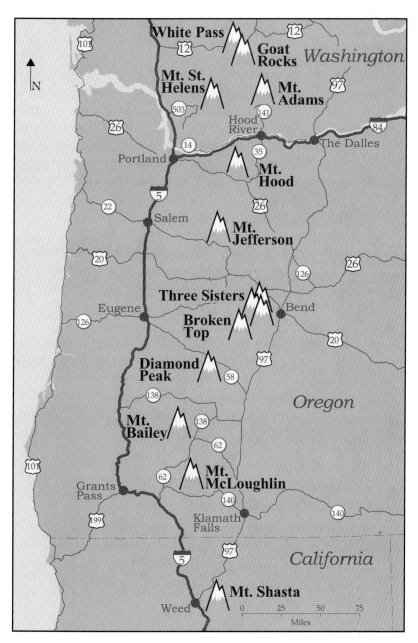

INTRODUCTION

How To Use This Guide

Organized by geographic location, *Oregon Descents* covers four distinct regions: Mt. Hood, Central Oregon, Southern Oregon and Southern Washington. Each section opens with a brief description of the area and offers an overview photograph. The photographs are included to help build your knowledge of the terrain and offer a perspective of the route if you are unfamiliar with the area. All routes described in this book are suggested routes for descent. The routes are recommended under safe conditions only; other lines, easier and more difficult, may exist. The photographs are one of many tools to aid in your evaluation of the terrain to be skied. *These routes are in no way a substitute for making your own evaluation of the slope and all ski routes should be evaluated for hazards prior to descent.* Every photograph includes a caption with the month the photograph was taken to help give a feel for the snow levels, but the snowpack will vary from year to year.

In addition to the photographs, every route is broken down into route statistics and route description. The route statistics include: season, difficulty rating, skiing vertical, starting and summit elevations, length and hazards. The rating system is defined by the length and technical nature of the access and by the terrain to be skied. All routes described in this book require at least an intermediate level of downhill skiing or boarding ability. The routes are rated as follows:

◆ **Intermediate** : Ability to link turns on moderate terrain (wide 15-25 degree slope) with good runout in consistent snow conditions. Basic understanding of map and compass. Basic knowledge of snowpack stability. The ability to recognize potential avalanche terrain.

◆ **Intermediate +** : Ability to link turns on moderate terrain (wide 15-25 degree slope) with good runout in *varied* snow con-

INTRODUCTION

ditions and use a kick turn to traverse. Confidence with a map and compass for access. Basic knowledge of snowpack stability. The ability to recognize potential avalanche terrain.

- **Advanced** : Ability to link turns on moderate to steep terrain (wide 20-35 degrees) with good runout in varied snow conditions. Good recovery from each turn and strong readiness for next turn. Glacier travel experience, knowledge of self-arrest techniques and ability to recognize dangerous crevassed terrain. Enjoy the challenge of access. Experienced with map and compass and solid understanding of avalanche dynamics.

- **Expert** : Comfortable with narrow and steep terrain (35-45 degrees). Ability to link short radius, accelerated turns on terrain with safe runout in varied conditions with immediate recovery and readiness for next turn. Alpine climbing experience. Knowledge of roped glacier travel and self-arrest techniques. Experienced route finding and working knowledge of avalanche conditions. Experience evaluating snowpack.

- **Expert +** : Solid climbing and skiing skills. Comfortable on all steep, exposed terrain. Knowledge of glacier travel, self arrest skills and experienced with snowpack evaluation. Instant recovery in turns, able to link jump turns and ski in all conditions. Expect to employ route finding skills and to evaluate snow conditions.

Seasonal Notes

Many of the routes included in *Oregon Descents* can be skied in a variety of seasons. For example, almost any route recommended for spring access could also be accessed in the winter during favorable snow conditions. The Northwest snowpack, however, lends itself to spring skiing. Wet, heavy, winter snows consolidate well, creating a stable, long lasting snowpack, yielding some of the best spring snow conditions in the country. Spring brings long days, blue skies and generally safer snow conditions than found in midwinter, all of which make spring trips very appealing. Winter access will almost always mean a longer trip requiring navigation skills, avalanche safety knowledge and, commonly, requires an overnight stay.

In general, the prime season for ski descents in the Northwest highcountry (over 8,000 feet) runs from April through July, while midwinter routes are commonly found below 8,000 feet. The spring and summer snowpack is typically more consistent and the access roads more clear of snow than in winter, allowing easier access and more enjoyable skiing. Skiing the high routes in midwinter requires allowing more time for approaches (often multiple days), more experience evaluating avalanche hazards, knowledge of weather patterns and recent temperatures in order to avoid the frustration of skiing crud and ice. Central Oregon often offers a more consistent and dryer winter snowpack than other Southern Cascade areas, making midwinter descents in the Central Cascades more rewarding than other Southern Cascade locations. Suggested 'best seasons' are included with each route. If an area is known for alternate seasons, this is noted but the route description is only given for the 'best season'.

Backcountry Access

The ever-growing popularity of off-piste' skiing is creating more conflicts between backcountry users, ski areas and the National Forest Service. Although only a small number of routes in *Oregon Descents* border on developed ski area terrain, all access our National Forests or other public lands. A growing number of areas now require permit fees, registration procedures

INTRODUCTION

and year-round trailhead parking permits to climb or ski. In our modern world, responsibility plays a major role in backcountry access. Entering the backcountry is not always restriction free and the user is responsibility for obtaining all necessary permits, following any registration requirements and using sound backcountry etiquette. Several state laws also apply to backcountry use. Backcountry travelers must understand the responsibilities which go along with access to our National Forests and public lands. Oregon and Washington laws are simple and assign responsibility where it belongs, on the backcountry user.

As applied to developed ski areas, Oregon's state law Section 30.985 (1) provides:

> *(a) Skiers who ski in any area not designated for skiing within the permit area assume the inherent risks thereof.*

As applied to wilderness travel and/or mountain climbing, Oregon's state law Section 401.615 provides:

> *(1). . . an individual who engages in wilderness travel or mountain climbing accepts and assumes the inherent risks of wilderness travel or mountain climbing.*

As applied to developed ski areas, Washington's state law, Section 70.117.020 provides:

> *(7) Any person skiing outside the confines of trails open for skiing or runs open for skiing within the ski area boundary shall be responsible for any injury or losses resulting from his or her action.*

These laws simply place liability on the skier. They do not impose criminal liability but could be used to make a lost or injured skier pay for any search and rescue work done on his or her behalf. In fact, Oregon state law supports charging lost or injured skiers or climbers up to five hundred dollars per individual for search and rescue work. The use of Forest Service hiker/climber registration is often necessary to receive a wilderness permit, and provides a safety backup should anything go wrong on your trip. Many registrations are unavailable or inactive in winter months so always leave your travel plans with friends or family and be safe, ski smart.

Although the legal responsibilities associated with backcountry access will probably never play a major role in your trips to the mountains, the more fundamental responsibilities associated with backcountry etiquette definitely will. It is with respect and restraint that we travel in the mountains. Leave no trace ethics apply in every season. Always use discretion when leaving human waste and if in doubt, pack it out. You are one of many users in the backcountry and everyone deserves the best possible experience.

One last thing to keep in mind when skiing in Oregon and Washington is the need for a sno-park permit. Required from November 15th through April 15th, this permit allows you to park in designated winter trailheads throughout both states. Permits are available daily or as an annual pass and Washington and Oregon have a reciprocal agreement, so your home state permit is valid in both states.

INTRODUCTION

Cascade Weather and Snow

Often referred to as 'Cascade Crud', the Northwest snowpack averages about 14% water in contrast to 6% or 8% water found in the snow of the Rockies[1]. Wet, dense snow can be very frustrating to the backcountry traveler and Cascade skiing is often best come spring consolidation. However, good snow can still be found in the winter. Background knowledge of Northwest weather patterns and storm cycles will help save you from frustrating trips in Cascade Crud.

Climbing above cloud level on Mt. St. Helens. May

1. http://members.aol.com/crockeraf/snoqlnet.htm, based on data since 1979.

The moisture content and density of the snow are directly related to air temperature and storm track. The colder the air, the lower the moisture content and the lighter (less dense) the snow. Armed with questions about storm basics, the snow conditions for a specific scenario can be determined. Important questions are:

- Where did the storm system originate?
- What is the current freezing level?
- When was the last snowfall?
- What is the exposure and elevation of your potential route?

Cascade storms can be simplified to about four different types or tracks: south-southwest, west-southwest, west-northwest, and northerly. Each storm track can be characterized and used to help anticipate snow conditions at a given location.

Storms out of the south-southwest (often referred to as the 'Pineapple Express') are characterized by warm temperatures and heavy precipitation. The warm South Pacific air masses bring high snow levels of approximately 8,000 feet or higher. The high snow levels cause rain in most mountain areas, rendering very poor skiing conditions and increased avalanche danger. A southerly storm can significantly reduce existing snow coverage and, when followed by colder air, will produce icy, crusty snow conditions.

More common are west-southwest systems. Influenced less by air from the South Pacific and more by air from the west, temperatures are cooler and the storms generate snow levels of approximately 4,000 - 7,000 feet depending on the season. A west-southwest storm can create reasonable snow conditions at Northwest area ski resorts.

The best winter ski conditions are produced by west-northwest and northerly storm tracks. Carrying cold air from the Gulf of Alaska, British Columbia or the Yukon, west-northwest and northerly systems are characterized by cold temperatures down to sea level. Snow levels associated with

INTRODUCTION

these systems range from sea level to 5,000 feet varying with the season.

Regardless of the storm track, better snow conditions are often found on routes east of the Cascade Crest because the air masses producing the storms cool significantly as they rise up the west side and move over the crest, dropping colder, lighter snow on the east side of the crest. The east slope, however, may not receive as much precipitation as the west slope because the storms often lose a majority of their moisture on the west side as the air mass is forced up the west slope. This phenomenon is often illustrated in higher snowfall reports at Mt. Hood's Timberline ski area than at the neighboring and more easterly located Mt. Hood Meadows ski area. The difference in snow accumulation amounts is more noticeable at areas not immediately part of the crest.

Snow conditions can be further enhanced when a storm is followed by evening or overnight clearing that causes overnight temperatures to remain or drop well below freezing, thus, 'drying out' the snowpack. However, this will only occur if the snowfall is already low in moisture content. Clear, cold weather following a warm wet storm will only cause hard, crusty con-

Altocumulus clouds, indicators of low pressure and poor weather

CASCADE WEATHER AND SNOW

ditions. North facing terrain often holds dry desirable snow longer than similar elevations with more southerly exposure where daytime temperatures warm the snowpack.

In addition to differentiating between storm systems, a few tips are helpful in understanding when and where to expect good snow. Understanding the freezing level and associated snow level of a storm is fundamental in determining snow conditions. The *freezing level* is simply the elevation at which the air reaches 32 degrees Fahrenheit, while the *snow level* is the elevation at which snow can be expected and is commonly 1,000 feet below the freezing level. Snow accumulation at the snow level is going to be wet, heavy Cascade Crud. The best snow conditions are found 1,000 - 2,000 feet above the freezing level or 2,000 - 3,000 feet above the snow level where air temperatures are 25 degrees Fahrenheit or below. Closely following weather reports for storm track and associated freezing levels allows a historical perspective of the snowpack and an understanding of current snow conditions to be developed.

Freezing level information is helpful for evaluating route choices. Rain and 40 degrees at low elevation can often mean good snow in the mountains. Air temperature typically falls with any gain in elevation and the average drop in air temperature is about 3.5 degrees Fahrenheit per 1,000 feet in elevation gain[2]. So, if the air temperature in Portland (400 feet elevation) is 40 degrees Fahrenheit and a ski route begins at 6,400 feet, the air temperature at the route can be estimated using the following equation:

$$\text{known temp.} - \frac{\text{elevation change} \times 3.5}{1,000} = \text{temp. at route elevation}$$

Using the data from the above scenario:

$$40° - \frac{6,000 \times 3.5}{1,000} = 40° - 21° = 19° \text{ at } 6,400 \text{ ft.}$$

Thus, if the temperature at one elevation, and the elevation of the ski route are known, an estimate of the snow conditions at the route can be made. The exception to this

[2]Renner, Jeff, *Northwest Mountain Weather*, Seattle; The Mountaineers, 1992

INTRODUCTION

equation occurs during an inversion, when cold moist air is trapped in valleys and lowlands under a warmer air mass, resulting in warmer temperatures at higher elevations than lower elevations. Keep an eye out for inversions in local forecasts. Accurate weather information is available from a variety of sources including weather radio, the World Wide Web, and ski resort snow report lines. See the Appendix for a list of weather information sources.

Early morning Lenticular cloud on the south side of Mt. Hood. May

Avalanche Awareness

Avalanches do not happen by accident. A natural series of events causes instability in the snowpack leading to avalanches. The events and how unstable the snowpack becomes depend on many variables. A backcountry traveler needs to know how to recognize conditions that lead to avalanches. Although not a replacement for experience, the following information is intended to aid in understanding and evaluating the snowpack.

Fundamental to avalanche dynamics is understanding that avalanches generally occur during or shortly after a change occurs to the snowpack. Avalanches are the result of slopes attempting to regain stability following a change in snowpack dynamics. Typically, the change is from a loading of the snowpack through added precipitation (rain or snow), wind transported snow, or solar radiation (sunshine). The final variable is often the load of a skier or boarder on the slope. Snow is dynamic and continually adjusts to any stress or change in the snow layers. The following scenarios are indicators for questioning snowpack stability.

- Heavy snows following a prolonged dry period, warm or cold.
- Heavy snows accompanied by high winds, watch lee slopes.
- Storms characterized by warming trends or followed by rain.
- Spring or winter snowfall with warm overnight temperatures and or warm sunshine, watch SE, W, SW slopes particularly in late afternoon.

Two general avalanche categories are of concern to Northwest skiers: loose snow avalanches and slab avalanches. Loose snow avalanches are characterized by the release of surface snow during or shortly after a storm cycle, and during warming trends such as rain or direct sunlight. Loose snow slides typically occur on terrain of 30 degrees or steeper but can occur at lesser angles. Often only a thin surface layer of snow, loose snow avalanches generally grow as they descend,

INTRODUCTION

gathering strength and speed. Loose snow avalanches are also capable of releasing larger slab avalanches. A very common form of loose snow avalanche in the Northwest is a wet snow sluff. Sluffs occur following intense sun and are very common in the spring snowpack of the Northwest. Sluffs commonly release along a skier or boarder's path. Although wet snow sluffs are not always particularly dangerous, they are capable of knocking a skier down or potentially sweeping a skier onto dangerous terrain and should be viewed as potentially hazardous.

In contrast to loose snow avalanches, slab avalanches are characterized by fracture lines and the movement of cohesive layers or slabs over a uniform sliding surface. Slab

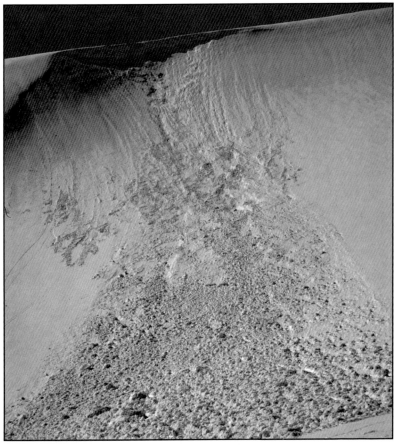

A loose snow slide (sluff) on Mt. St. Helens. May

avalanches are the most dangerous avalanche to backcountry travelers because they release and travel quickly. Most common on slopes between 30 and 45 degrees, slabs can occur on slopes ranging from 20 - 50 degrees, given the right conditions.

Although slabs very in depth, size and snow type, slab avalanches are dangerous regardless of size or depth of the snow. Slabs release when a weak layer in the snowpack fails, causing the cohesive slab layers above to slide. Release may be the result of a collapsed snow layer due to added weight or stress of new snow, rain or a skier. Fundamental to slab avalanches is the sliding surface or bed under the slab. Sliding surfaces in the Northwest are often the result of the formation of an ice layer or lens between snow layers. Warm temperatures, wet snow or rain followed by cooler air can produce an ideal surface for new snow to build on and given the right loading, lead to slab avalanches. Cold storms dumping snow on a frozen crust or old snow surface can produce conditions that lead to slab avalanches. Additionally, classic slab formation is associated with high winds and the formation of slabs due to wind transported snow onto leeward slopes.

A slab avalanche in upper Heather Canyon. April   Photo: *Jeff Schuh*

INTRODUCTION

Northwest skiers and climbers must be equally, if not more, avalanche conscious in the spring as in winter. Spring storms often dump large amounts of wet snow, that, followed by sunny spring weather, results in hazardous avalanche conditions. During sunny spring weather, the avalanche hazard is generally lowest during the night and early morning hours when temperatures are cooler and the snowpack remains frozen. In contrast, intense solar radiation and warm air temperatures during mid to late day weakens surface snow layers, thus, increases the avalanche hazard. Spring slide activity generally starts on southeast facing slopes receiving morning sun and moves to west and southwest aspects as the day progresses. Snow stability is also affected by any cloud cover during the night or by warm (above freezing) air temperatures overnight. The lack of overnight freezing allows the snowpack to weaken at progressively deeper layers in the snow cover. Backcountry travelers need to use continued caution throughout the spring season.

Regardless of season or avalanche type, avalanche evaluation is a process based on the continual collection of information from your surroundings. Having an historical perspective of the snowpack, either through first hand analysis or through reading detailed reports over the course of the winter, is a great way of keeping track of conditions. On any given slope, the snowpack and avalanche potential will commonly vary from place to place within the slope. Attention should always be paid to signals from nature around you. Other slide activity in the area, cracks propagating along a slope, small slabs breaking under foot or ski, settling or wumpfing noises in the snowpack, large cornices, wind scoured slopes, and convex slope features are all natural signs that avalanche conditions may exist. Three questions that should always be considered are:

- ◆ Is the terrain capable of avalanche?
- ◆ Is the weather (past or present) contributing to instability?
- ◆ Are you in the path of any potential slide activity?

A yes answer to any of these questions should be followed by further investigation that includes: alternative route choices, ski cutting the slope or further snowpack analysis such as a snow pit, shovel shear or a Rutschblock test. Being prepared for travel in avalanche terrain means staying aware of conditions and carrying the necessary tools for further investigation and necessary emergency action. At a minimum, avalanche tools should include, a current avalanche report, a partner, a shovel, a probe, avalanche beacons and knowledge of how to use these.

Several avalanche hot lines can be used in the Northwest and a variety of good books are available on the subject. More recently the World Wide Web has become an excellent resource for reading detailed snowpack analysis and gaining a general understanding of current conditions. See the Appendix for specific source information. Remember, existing tracks on a slope do not always mean the slope is safe.

Equipment

Backcountry ski and snowboard equipment has improved significantly in the past five years. The growing demand for gear that meets the needs of today's more aggressive skiing styles has led to the plastic telemark boot revolution and the availability of backcountry skis designed with stiff, responsive boots in mind. Similarly, the development of lightweight, easy to use snowshoes and packs designed to carry snowboards have helped fuel backcountry snowboard access.

The advent of plastic telemark boots and the ability to use plastic mountaineering boots in snowboard setups have allowed telemarkers and boarders to confidently access terrain once reserved for alpine touring or randonee' skiers. The use of heavy-duty boots with buckles or plastic telemark boots is recommended for many routes in *Oregon Descents*. The multiple buckle and plastic telemark boots available today give superior ski control and are necessary for the wider, more stable telemark skis. Crampons are needed for several routes described in this book and the use of heavy duty or plastic telemark boots allows for safe travel on terrain where crampons are necessary. Several of the high country routes recommended here commonly require crampons for early morning ascents, while the afternoon sun softens the route for a ski descent.

Today's skis offer a wide variety of choices. Regardless of brand name, all the new telemark skis are wider than ever. Once reserved for powder and randonee' boards, ski widths of 85-100 mm are now common for skis marketed as 'tele' skis, but 100 mm is on the wide side for typical snowpack. The wider skis allow for greater stability and flotation in all conditions. Good benchmark dimensions are now commonly considered to be 82-97 mm at the tip and 75-85 mm at the tail with about 20 mm of side cut (the difference between the ski's tip width and the ski's center width). The wide dimensions lend themselves to the maritime snowpack and are versatile enough to meet the needs of ski mountaineering. Generally, the wider ski dimensions allow you to ski a shorter length ski. The general trend is to ski a shorter ski hard, rather than to ski a longer board caution.

EQUIPMENT

Many telemark skiers find that heavier, stiffer boots allow skiing boards once reserved for randonee' setups, although, with the new, wider tele-board dimensions, the line between randonee' and telemark skis is getting thin.

In addition to skis and boots, the backcountry traveler needs climbing aids. Traditionally, three methods of uphill travel are used in the backcountry. These are skins, crampons and boot packing or step kicking. Skins are most commonly used in winter conditions with average to dry snow. The most common skins are synthetic mohair with an adhesive base. Skins should match the width of the ski. Narrow skins on a wide ski will not climb as well as a wider skin matched to the ski. Snowboarders commonly use snowshoes in midwinter conditions and the snowshoe market grows every year.

When spring consolidation occurs, most routes are accessed without the need for skins or snowshoes. More common in the spring and summer months is kicking steps. The consolidated spring snowpack offers firm footing and quick travel. A majority of spring and summer routes can be done by hiking; however, spring storms and warm weather that frequently create soft, post holing conditions should be a concern. It pays to carry skins or snowshoes as backup given new snowfall or the access road condition is unknown. Similarly, routes requiring long access may be best served by skins or snowshoes.

An exception to kicking steps is hard pack or icy conditions requiring crampons. Crampons are often necessary on high routes in the winter and are common on spring routes when the overnight freezing levels cause the snowpack to firm up and often not soften until midday. Most step-in crampons sold today fit telemark ski boots. Crampons are recommended for several routes and are noted in the route descriptions. Ice axes are also commonly used on several routes. Generally, if crampons are needed to climb, an axe should be carried for self-arrest.

A final piece of equipment which is often very helpful is an altimeter. Altimeters can be invaluable tools in following snow covered approach trails and are equally as useful above timberline and in poor weather conditions.

MT. HOOD

Mt. Hood from the north, cloud level 6,000 feet. September

PART I
MT. HOOD AREA

At 11,239 feet, Mt. Hood is the highest peak in Oregon. Said to be one of the most climbed glaciated peaks in the world, Mt. Hood is a familiar icon in the Northwest outdoor community and the backbone of Northwest Oregon skiing. Thanks to Mt. Hood, Oregon holds skiable snow twelve months out of the year. Every season on Mt. Hood has its own special places and snow conditions.

The mountain has three primary access points for skiing: the south side via Timberline Road, the east side via Hood River Meadows and the north side via Cloud Cap and Cooper Spur. Each area has its own personality and serves different ski objectives. The south side offers the easiest access. Featuring broad open slopes, the south side is the most widely used area on Mt. Hood. The Hood River Meadows area is less traveled and serves the upper and lower reaches of White River and Heather Canyons primarily for winter skiing below timberline or spring skiing above timberline. The north side is a popular summer access area and offers the finest summer skiing on the mountain as well as good winter and spring skiing.

In addition to Mt. Hood, the surrounding Hood National Forest offers a variety of smaller ridges and peaks to ski. One of the best is Tom, Dick and Harry Mountain just west of Mt. Hood. Tom, Dick and Harry is included at the start of the Mt. Hood section.

Sunrise on the south side. May

TOM, DICK AND HARRY MOUNTAIN

Tom, Dick and Harry Ridge from the north. January

Route Information
- **Season** - December through March
- **Difficulty** - Intermediate to expert
- **Total Skiing Vertical** - 1,000 ft.
- **Starting Elevation** - 3,400 ft.
- **Summit or Goal** - 5,040 ft.
- **Length** - 1 Day, 4-6 hours
- **Hazards** - High avalanche potential in upper bowls

Getting There
- **Access** - The Mirror Lake Sno-park is located 0.8 of a mile west of Ski Bowl on State Route 26.
- **Trailhead** - Mirror Lake Sno-park / Wind Creek Trail # 664

TOM, DICK & HARRY

◆ **Map/Information-** Geo-Graphics Mt. Hood Wilderness Map, Zig Zag Ranger District - 503-622-5741

Tom, Dick and Harry Mountain is a beautiful alpine ridge southeast of Mt. Hood offering some of the steepest terrain in the Hood area. Although the route can suffer from its low elevation, the skiing is hard to beat when the snow level has been consistently below 3,000 feet. The close proximity to Portland and small size of the area does mean the ridge sees a lot of skier traffic. The west end offers great intermediate terrain, while the main ridge holds excellent steeper terrain with several chutes along the cliff band. The cliff area is also subject to high risk of avalanche so be sure to check the local avalanche conditions (503-326-2400) before skiing the upper ridgeline.

The area can be accessed in two different ways. The simplest method is to follow the Wind Creek Trail from the Mirror Lake Sno-park just west of Ski Bowl on Route 26. The trail is about two miles long and switchbacks up to the western end of the ridge. The ridge overlooks Mirror Lake and offers a wide variety of skiable terrain. The western end of the ridge (climber's right) allows low angle access and offers good intermediate skiing. Higher on the ridge, the terrain ranges from advanced to expert plus. Several cliff bands create a variety of narrow chutes and steep terrain extremely susceptible to avalanche. Exit via the same route used for access or for a few extra turns hike the ridge to the ski area and ski out through the lift served area. Although the Wind Creek Trail offers easy access, it is often well traveled and is notoriously difficult to descend due to tight trees and narrow switchbacks.

Alternatively, access can be begun from the Ski Bowl parking lot. Using the Ski Bowl access is best done early in the morning before the area opens. The eastern reaches of Tom, Dick and Harry are actually accessible by a short hike from Ski Bowl's upper lift. Marketed as the *Outback,* this area is patrolled by the ski area and as a result is often skied out by lift served skiers. Given early season snowfall and on occasions when Ski Bowl is closed, the eastern bowls offer excellent skiing.

PART ONE MT. HOOD

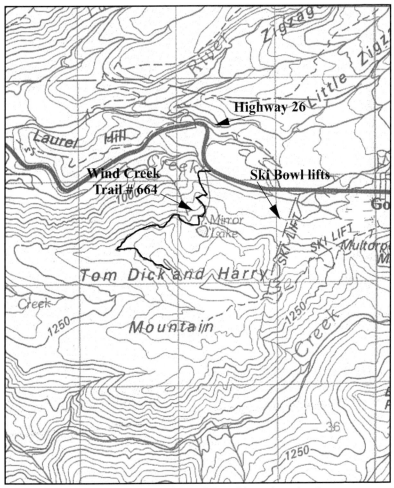

Tom, Dick and Harry on the USGS Bull Run Map, elevation in meters

Turns on the upper section of Tom, Dick and Harry. January

MT. HOOD SOUTH SIDE ROUTES
USING THE PALMER CHAIR FOR SOUTH SIDE ACCESS

The south side of Mt. Hood is far from a traditional wilderness experience. The area is dominated by Timberline Ski Area's chair lifts. Riding the Palmer chair, however, is an access option for any of the south side routes.

Timberline offers a one-ride climber's ticket for ten dollars. Riding the lift puts you at 8,540 feet but requires starting at seven or eight am, considerably later than many parties feel is safe to climb Hood. Riding the lift is a good option when the freezing levels are low and allow quick travel on firm snow or when reaching the summit is not the goal. A few conditions also apply to Timberline's climber ticket. Timberline will not sell you a ticket unless you carry a cellular phone or a Mt. Hood Locator Unit (MLU). Climber's registration is required and climber tickets are only available during the first hour of operation. The MLU is an emergency signal beacon designed solely for use on Mt. Hood's south side. They can be rented from the Mt. Hood Inn in Government Camp 24 hours a day (503-272-3205) or from Portland mountain shops such as Oregon Mountain Community, The Mountain Shop and REI.

Typically, the Palmer chair is open consistently from April through June or July. Hours of operation vary but, generally, the chair begins running at 8 am in the early spring and moves to 7 am by June. Be sure to call Timberline (503-222-2211) for the latest information.

Looking south from the top of the Palmer Chair, 8,540 feet Mt. Hood. May

MT. HOOD - SOUTH SIDE

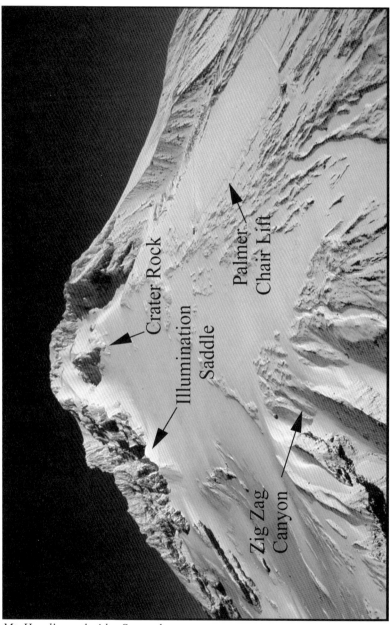

Mt. Hood's south side. September

MT. HOOD
ALPINE AND GLADE TRAILS

A rare powder day on Mt. Hood. January

Route Information

- **Season** - December through March
- **Difficulty** - Intermediate
- **Total Skiing Vertical** - 1,600 ft.
- **Starting Elevation** - 4,000 ft.
- **Summit or Goal** - 5,600 ft.
- **Length** - 1 Day
- **Hazards** - Minimal

Getting There

- **Access** - To access the top of either trail, follow the Timberline Mt. Road turn off from highway 26 near Government Camp and drive 6 miles to Timberline Lodge. Begin at the Timberline Ski Area. Alternatively, to access the bottom of the Glade trail, take the

ALPINE AND GLADE TRAILS

Government Camp Loop Road off of Highway 26. Follow the loop road to the Huckleberry Inn. Head north on Blossom road just West of the inn. The end of this road is where the Glade Trail meets Government camp.

◆ **Trailhead** - To begin at the top use Timberline Lodge. To begin at the base of the Glade use the unmarked trail at the end of Blossom road in Government Camp.

◆ **Map/Information** - Geo-Graphics - Mt. Hood Wilderness, Green Trails Mt. Hood # 462, USGS Mt. Hood South, Zig Zag Ranger District - 503-622-5741.

The Alpine and Glade Trails are remnants of the early days of Mt. Hood lift skiing. Today, they are commonly used by skiers and boarders from the Timberline Ski Area who are returning to Government Camp or are trying to get in a longer run. Both trails lead from the base of the lower lifts of Timberline to the Government Camp area. The trails offer good runs through small meadows and forest. Mellow terrain is balanced out by narrow sections and often varied snow conditions. The elevation change between Timberline to Government Camp is often a critical zone with regard to snow quality, but when the temperature in Government Camp is cold and snow has freshly fallen, both trails are worthy of a couple laps.

The most common way of skiing either trail is to begin at the Timberline Ski Area. Skiing either route from the top requires either hiking back up, hitchhiking, or leaving a second car in Government Camp for the return to Timberline. Both trails are short enough to allow at least a couple of laps in a day. Another option is to begin in Government Camp and hike up first. This is best done on the Glade trail. The trail does not see a whole lot of uphill traffic so be prepared to encounter people on the descent who may be surprised to see you.

Both trails begin near the base of the Blossom lift. Blossom is the western most lift on the mountain. The Glade Trail begins just west of the Alpine Trail and intermittently follows a powerline cut down to Government Camp. The Alpine Trail connects Timberline to the Summit Ski Hill at the east end of Government Camp and can be used to access the

West Leg Ski Trail, that is shown as the Old Timberline Road on most maps. The West Leg Ski Trail can then be used to ski to the current Timberline access road for return to your vehicle.

The Glade Trail is very straight forward and offers only limited route options while the Alpine Trail offers a wider variety of connecting routes to extend your tour once down below 4,500 feet. Consult a map or Klindt Vielbig's book, *Cross-Country Ski Routes of Oregon's Cascades*, for more touring options in the Government camp area. Either route can also be used in conjunction with any of the higher routes on the south side of Mt. Hood to make for a longer ski descent, but complicating return logistics.

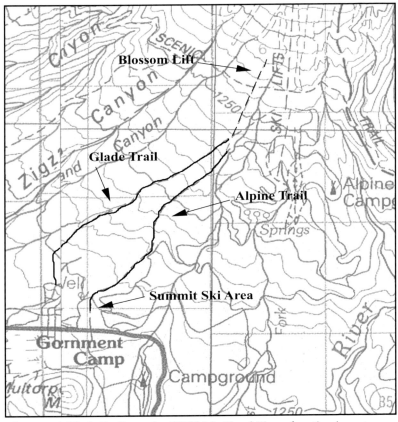

Alpine and Glade Trails on the USGS Mt. Hood Map, elevation in meters

MT. HOOD - CIRCUMNAVIGATION

Heading north across the Sandy Glacier near 8,500 feet. May

Route Information

- **Season** - May
- **Difficulty** - Expert +
- **Starting Elevation** - 5,900 ft.
- **Summit or Goal** - Traverse at 8,600 ft.
- **Length** - 1 Day
- **Hazards** - Glacier travel, high crevasse hazard, rockfall, moderate avalanche potential

Getting There

- **Access** - From Highway 26 in Government Camp, take the Timberline Mt. Road turn off and drive 6 miles to Timberline Lodge. Access is directly from Timberline Lodge parking lot. *Be sure to sign in at the climber*

registration area at the Wy' east Day Lodge area (available 24 hours a day).
- ◆ **Trailhead** - South Side Climber's trail at the base of the Palmer Glacier, Palmer Chair lift
- ◆ **Map/Information** - Geo-Graphics - Mt. Hood Wilderness, Green Trails Mt. Hood # 462, USGS Mt. Hood South, Zig Zag Ranger District - 503-622-5741

Not exactly a ski descent, the circumnavigation of Mt. Hood is a classic Hood adventure. First completed in the 1930's, the circumnavigation tour gives you an intimate sense of the mountain and is great test of your ski mountaineering skills. The tour crosses ten glaciers, climbs six significant ridgelines and gives a new sense of awe for Mt. Hood. A true mountaineering objective, the circumnavigation of Hood requires roped glacier travel and varied climbing and skiing skills. The seasonal time window best for the circumnavigation is short. Go too early in the season and rime ice on the ridges and deceivingly well covered crevasses complicate the trip; go too late and poor snow conditions, lack of snow on several ridges and very exposed crevasse fields will slow travel. In average snow years, May is probably the best month. The snow coverage is still good, the large dangerous crevasses are beginning to show their breadth, but the ridges are still relatively easy to cross. This route is not the time to practice mountaineering skills but requires solid expert skills to allow a good pace. Be prepared to ski roped, set up belays and use ice tools as well as crampons.

The best route is clockwise around the mountain at about 8,600 feet beginning on the south side above the Palmer chair. On the route, elevation will vary depending on snow levels, crevasse exposure and your own judgment, but the terrain lends itself to a route between about 8,600 and 7,600 feet. Most of the glacial headwalls are near the 8,600 foot level and elevation is best held as near to 8,600 feet as possible. Either hike to the top of the Palmer chair or ride the lift to begin the tour. (See information about riding the Palmer chair at start of south side section.) If hiking to the top of the Palmer is chosen, follow the climber's trail just east (climber's right) of the groomed runs on Palmer Glacier. The trail is packed out by a snow cat to keep climbers off the groomed runs. Be sure to stay well away from Timberline's grooming machines and skiers. The climber's route goes past the Silcox Hut (7,000 feet) and stays to the east (climber's right) of the groomed slopes.

Once above the Palmer, head west (left) across the Zigzag Glacier toward Illumination Rock. Access to the Reid Glacier is recommended below Illumination Rock, so drop a couple hundred feet and aim for the low side of Illumination Rock. Crossing above Illumination Rock is also possible but with good snow conditions taking the high route is not necessary. Down climb onto the Reid, traverse directly below the icefall and make a dash for Yocum Ridge. Yocum Ridge can be negotiated at about 8,500 feet without any technical concerns.

Traversing east toward the Coe Glacier. May

PART ONE - MT. HOOD

Once on Yocum Ridge, the Sandy Glacier is the next crossing and with the right snow conditions posses no real difficulties. The Sandy Headwall looms above and descending a few hundred feet on the Sandy may be necessary to avoid crevasses or rockfall debris.

Cathedral Ridge is the next obstacle and like Yocum Ridge, should be crossed near 8,500 feet. Prepare to regain some elevation to cross Cathedral Ridge if the traverse of the Sandy Glacier required any descent. Be sure to be well past the Sandy headwall and out of any direct rockfall line before climbing. Gaining Cathedral Ridge puts you above the Glisan Glacier and headed onto the Coe and Ladd Glaciers. Prepare to negotiate a fairly complex crevasses system on the Coe and Ladd Glaciers. Again, hold as much elevation as possible. A high route between 8,400 and 9,000 feet will allow crossing the next ridge just below Pulpit Rock with minimal additional climbing. Two options are available for crossing at Pulpit Rock but the higher the elevation, the better. Again, 8,500 to 8,600 feet seems to be the magic number. Gaining the ridge at Pulpit Rock puts you on the northwest side of the Snow Dome just west of the Elliot Glacier. The Elliot will most likely require the greatest loss of elevation to cross safely, unless a higher more technical line is chosen. Either way, you must ascend the Cooper Spur Ridge to 'Tie In Rock' at 8,600 feet.

From Cooper Spur, continue around onto the Newton Clark Glacier. Traverse Newton Clark around 8,300 feet to avoid seracs higher, but stay above 8,000 feet to avoid crevasses and to stay above Heather Canyon. The Newton Clark Glacier yields to the White River Glacier and provides a path back to the start. The best place to regain the Palmer Glacier is between 7,600 and 7,800 feet. Do not drop much below 7,600 feet so you can meet the Palmer chair and complete the traverse within 1,000 vertical feet of the start. Be sure to sign back in at the climber registry.

MT. HOOD - CRATER ROCK

Upper south side and Crater Rock. September

Route Information

- **Season** - Winter, Spring, Early Summer
- **Difficulty** - Intermediate
- **Total Skiing Vertical** - 3,000 ft.
- **Starting Elevation** - 5,900 ft.
- **Summit or Goal** - 9,300 ft.
- **Length** - 1/2 to 1 Day
- **Hazards** - Moderate avalanche, low visibility in poor weather, deceptive fall-line

Getting There

- **Access** - From Highway 26 in Government Camp, take the Timberline Mt. Road turn off and drive 6 miles to Timberline Lodge. Access is directly from Timberline

Lodge parking lot. *Be sure to sign in at the climber registration area at the Wy' East Day Lodge (available 24 hours a day).*

- **Trailhead -** South Side Climber's trail at the base of the Palmer Glacier, Palmer Chair lift
- **Map/Information -** Geo-Graphics - Mt. Hood Wilderness, Green Trails Mt. Hood # 462, USGS Mt. Hood South, Zig Zag Ranger District - 503-622-5741

Although far from a wilderness experience, the south side of Mt. Hood holds several good skiing options and is a source of skiable snow for most of the year. It may seem odd to hike along the groomed runs of the Timberline Ski Area, but once you are beyond the final lift tower of the Palmer Chair, the mountain takes on a new personality and sense of scale.

The Crater Rock/Hogsback area holds snow much of the year. Access distance is the same regardless of season because the Timberline Road is open year round and, until late summer, the south side is skiable down to Timberline Lodge. Of course conditions vary; winter access often yields hardpack and wind scoured slopes, although the right winter conditions will yield powder. Spring and summer yield corn snow for which Mt. Hood is famous.

Crater Rock is the obvious large rock outcropping in the middle of the south side just below the summit. Climbing to the elevation of Crater Rock and the Hogsback puts you about 1,000 vertical feet from the summit of Hood. This is the main thoroughfare to the summit. A clear spring day will commonly see upwards of one hundred people in this area. The Hogsback is also a great place to begin a ski descent after reaching the summit if the upper pitch through the Old Chute is not appealing. The Hogsback and Crater Rock area offer a variety of terrain steeper than the remainder of the descent. The upper sections should be skied with caution because the pitches leading down from the Hogsback often contain small crevasses and sink holes which are not always obvious.

To access Crater Rock and the Hogback, follow the climber's trail just east (climber's right) of the groomed runs on

Palmer Glacier. Again, the trail here is packed out by a snow cat to keep climbers off the groomed runs. Be sure to stay well away from Timberline's grooming machines and skiers. The cat drivers are not sympathetic to folks climbing up their freshly groomed runs. The climber's route goes past the Silcox Hut (7,000 feet) and stays to the east (climber's right) of the groomed slopes. Continue to above the Palmer chair lift (8,560 feet). Over the course of the winter, the snow cats build up a wall of snow at the top of the upper lift that can be avoided by a short traverse to the left or right from the upper lift tower. Remember this wall during the descent! Once above the lift, head for the right side of Crater Rock and pick a line of ascent. Crampons and an ice axe are recommended.

    A word of caution for the descent; the fall line from the base of Crater Rock can lead a disoriented skier toward either White River or Zig Zag Canyon. Skiing into either canyon is not recommended. Both Canyons have avalanche prone terrain and neither returns skiers to the Timberline parking area. Attempting a descent during conditions of poor visibility has lead many climbers off their intended routes. As with any backcountry trip, all skiers should carry a map and compass as well as, have the knowledge to use them.

PART ONE - MT. HOOD

MT. HOOD - ILLUMINATION SADDLE

Looking at the south side, Zig Zag Canyon in the foreground and Illumination Saddle above. September

Route Information

- **Season** - December through August
- **Difficulty** - Intermediate, Advanced in winter
- **Total Skiing Vertical** - 3,000 ft.
- **Starting Elevation** - 6,000 ft.
- **Summit or Goal** - 9,300 ft.
- **Length** - ½ to 1 Day
- **Hazards** - Moderate avalanche, low visibility in poor weather, deceptive fall-line

Getting There

- **Access** - From Highway 26 in Government Camp take the Timberline Mt. Road turn off and head toward Timberline Lodge. Access is directly from Timberline Lodge parking lot. *Be sure to sign in at the climber*

ILLUMINATION SADDLE

registration area at the Wy' East Day Lodge area (available 24 hours a day).

- **Trailhead** - South Side Climber's trail at the base of the Palmer Glacier
- **Map/Information** - Geo-Graphics - Mt. Hood Wilderness, Green Trails Mt. Hood # 462, USGS Mt. Hood South, Zig Zag Ranger District - 503-622-5741

Illumination Saddle is a fun day ski from Timberline Lodge. The terrain is moderate and the ascent nontechnical. Illumination Saddle can also be skied as part of a descent from a south side climb. The snow from Illumination Saddle and below is often softer than the pitches above leading to the summit and, thus, more skiable. The approach information is virtually the same as that for Crater Rock so be sure to read the introduction to the Crater Rock route. Illumination Saddle differs in that the elevation is about a thousand feet lower and is far enough from the south side climbing route to be less traveled than the Crater Rock route.

To access Illumination Saddle, follow the climbers trail just east (climber's right) of the groomed runs on Palmer Glacier. Remain parallel with the lift until the upper lift tower is reached. The trail is packed out by a snow cat to keep climbers off the groomed runs. Be sure to stay well away from Timberline's grooming machines and skiers. Once above the lift tower (8,560 feet), traverse west (climber's left) to access the slopes above. Head almost due north toward the large rock outcropping west (left) of the summit, this is Illumination Rock. A short steep pitch can be skied by climbing the slopes of Illumination Rock or ski the more moderate pitch from the saddle. The slopes below are wide open and, aside from a few rolls, hold a consistent, moderate pitch for 3,000 vertical feet. In high snow years and midwinter the saddle is steeper in pitch than at other times. Crampons and an ice axe are recommended for the ascent, particularly in winter.

A word of caution for the descent: following the fall line straight down from the saddle leads into Zig Zag Canyon and drops far below Timberline Lodge. Skiing down into the

PART ONE - MT. HOOD

canyon is not recommended. The head of the canyon cliffs out, holds avalanche prone slopes and should not be skied by anyone unfamiliar with the canyon topography. Attempting a descent from Illumination Saddle during conditions of poor visibility is dangerous and has caused many experienced climbers to lose their route. As with any backcountry trip, all skiers should be equipped with map and compass as well as, the ability to use them.

Turns descending from Illumination Saddle. October *Photo: Jeff Schuh*

MT. HOOD - SUMMIT SKI ROUTES

Looking up from the Hogsback, climbers are headed up main chute, Mazama route is on far left, Old Chute is near the center. June

Route Information

- **Season** - March through June
- **Difficulty** - Expert +
- **Starting Elevation** - 5,850 ft.
- **Summit or Goal** - 11,239 ft.
- **Length** - 1 Day
- **Hazards** - Glacier travel, moderate avalanche, low visibility in poor weather, deceptive fall-line

Getting There

- **Access** - From Highway 26 in Government Camp, take the Timberline Mt. Road turn off and head toward Timberline Lodge. Access is directly from Timberline Lodge parking lot. *Be sure to sign in at the climber*

PART ONE - MT HOOD

registration in the Wy' East Day Lodge (available 24 hours a day).

- **Trailhead** - South Side Climber's trail at the base of the Palmer Glacier
- **Map/Information** - Geo-Graphics - Mt. Hood Wilderness, Green Trails Mt. Hood # 462, USGS Mt. Hood South, Zig Zag Ranger District - 503-622-5741

Skiing from the summit of Mt. Hood is most accessible via the south side climbing route. Although the climb up the south side is considered by most to be a novice glacier climb, skiing the south side from the summit is not for the novice. The summit pitch is exposed to the bergschrund, does not offer a safe run out until it drops below the Hogsback and the angle varies between 40 and 50 degrees depending on location and snowpack. The route is, however, quite skiable given good conditions. Several chutes on the south side can be skied and all lead to the same open pitch above the bergschrund. The first chute to climber's left (Old Chute) of the main climbing chute is often the first to soften enough to allow an edge to hold but is one of the narrowest options. The wide chute further to the west (Mazama Route) is a popular option, but often remains firm well into the afternoon even on a calm sunny day. Whichever chute is chosen, be sure to know the status of the bergschrund below. By June, the bergschrund is often exposed along the area below the chutes and a safe line is essential.

Although the south side climbing route is very accessible, the route involves glacier travel, crevasse exposure and the use of crampons, axe and roped travel. Two options are available for the ascent. The most common method is to hike from the Timberline Lodge parking area. This ascent follows the climber's trail just east (climber's right) of the groomed runs on Palmer Glacier. The trail is packed out by a snowcat to keep climbers off the groomed runs. The climber's route goes past the Silcox Hut (7,000 feet) and stays east of the groomed slopes. Continue on the climber's trail to above the Palmer chair lift (8,560 feet). Once above the lift, head for the right side of Crater Rock and climb up to the Hogsback. The section from the Hogback to the summit is the true glacier travel section and involves negotiating the bergschrund. Depending on the snowpack and time of year, either traverse around the bergschrund or cross it on a snow bridge. Be sure to eye the pitch to climber's left for your descent. Take note of any exposed crevasses in preparation for your descent.

Once on the summit, you may need to wait for the snow conditions to soften up depending on your preferences. The upper pitch will begin to corn by noon on a warm spring day. The different descent options can be accessed and previewed by following the summit ridgeline west looking for a suitable descent line.

Another option for access is riding the Palmer chair lift to 8,600 feet. See the Palmer chair access information at the start of the south side section. Riding the chair should only be an option if the snow remains firm, lessening ice and rockfall danger and allowing quick travel.

Looking up at the Old Chute. June

Looking down the Old Chute from the summit. June

MT. HOOD - EAST SIDE ROUTES

The east side of Mt. Hood is dominated by the White River and Newton Clark Glaciers. The glaciers have created several large drainages accessible to skiers. There is talk about east side winter snows being lighter and 'better' than west side snow. Although this statement may have some validity, these two regions are so close to the crest that the difference is often negligible.

Aside from Mt. Hood Meadows Ski Area, the east side of Hood is less traveled than the south side. The terrain in the upper reaches of the drainages is prone to high avalanche potential and the upper flanks of the mountain are a serious undertaking in any snow conditions. The routes described here range from the easily accessible lower reaches of White River Canyon to the expert descent on the Wy'east climbing route. During midwinter the lower tree lined slopes of the Clark and Newton Creek drainages also yield good turns.

The east side of Mt. Hood, White River Glacier on the left, Newton Clark on the right. July Photo: Steve Boyer

PART ONE - MT. HOOD

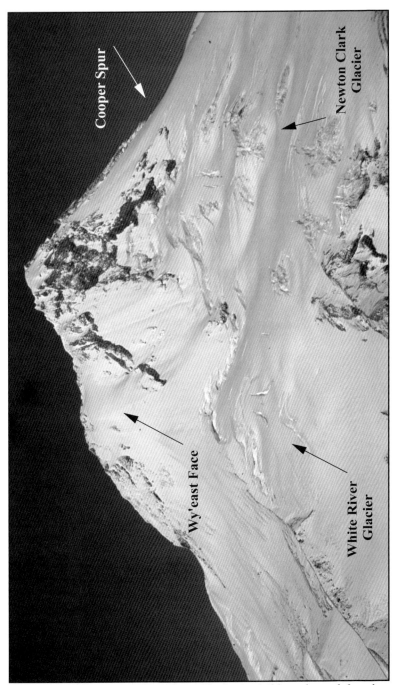

Mt. Hood from the east, the Palmer Glacier is visible on lower left and Cooper Spur follows the right side skyline. September

MT. HOOD - HEATHER CANYON

Heather Canyon above Mt. Hood Meadows Resort. July

Route Information

- **Season** – December through June
- **Difficulty** - Intermediate + to Expert
- **Total Skiing Vertical** – 2,000 – 3,000 ft.
- **Starting Elevation** – 5,300 ft.
- **Summit or Goal** – 7,000 – 8,000 ft.
- **Length** - 1 Day
- **Hazards** - Moderate to high avalanche danger, stream crossings on the approach.

Getting There

- **Access** - From Highway 26, continue two miles past Government Camp following the Highway 35 split and signs for Hood River and Mt. Hood Meadows Ski Area. Follow Highway 35 for seven more miles to the Mt. Hood

Meadows Ski Area turnoff. Continue on Highway 35 past the first entrance and take the second or lower entrance for Hood River Meadows Sno-park.
- **Trailhead** – Hood River Meadows Sno-park
- **Map/Information** - Geo-Graphics - Mt. Hood Wilderness, Green Trails Mt. Hood # 462, USGS quad Mt. Hood South. Zig Zag Ranger District - 503-622-5741

Heather Canyon runs along the northeast side of the Mt. Hood Meadows ski area. The upper canyon is served by the Heather Canyon Chair lift and is within the ski area boundary. The upper canyon is best skied either pre or post ski season when the ski area is closed. The lower canyon, however, does offer good winter terrain. The canyon is notoriously avalanche prone during winter months and is best avoided during periods of high avalanche danger. Heather Canyon can be combined with the Wy'east route for an excellent spring descent of over 5,000 vertical feet in length.

A side canyon off the Clark Creek drainage, Heather Canyon follows northwest of Clark Creek. The canyon is accessed via the Hood River Meadows lot (the nordic ski center lot). From the parking lot, follow the trail into the forest from the north side of the parking lot to the Clark Creek drainage and follow the creek northwest to treeline. At this point, a couple miles from the sno-park, you are looking into Heather Canyon. Several options can be skied from here. The left side ridgeline leads up to the Mt. Hood Meadows ski area with shots back into the canyon. The right side ridges also hold good terrain and lead to the next drainage to the east. Several good shots can found both in the trees and above treeline. Much of the terrain is accessed by lift served skiers and you need to be alert for skiers descending the canyon in both the upper and lower regions. A hazard to keep in mind during early season trips is stream crossings. Early season snowpack does not always cover the creek and makes for a difficult approach.

A second approach option is via the Mt. Hood Meadows Ski Area. This is only an option in spring when the area is closed for the season. Once closed for the season, the ski area lot is often gated so park at the gate and begin your hike from the main lot (5,300 feet). The easiest terrain to hike is along the west side of the area. Hiking the west side may not be the most direct but is the most gradual. Simply follow the lower lifts up to midmountain and the base of the upper chair. From the upper chair, continue to climb and head northeast toward Heather Canyon. A short traverse from the top of the upper chair brings you to the head of the Canyon.

The upper reaches of Heather Canyon seen from the northeast. April Photo: Jeff Schuh

PART ONE - MT. HOOD

MT. HOOD - WHITE RIVER CANYON

White River Canyon from treeline. November

Route Information

- **Season** - December through May
- **Difficulty** - Intermediate to Advanced
- **Total Skiing Vertical** - 1,000 - 2,000 ft.
- **Starting Elevation** - 4,250 ft.
- **Summit or Goal** - Varies
- **Length** - 1 Day
- **Hazards** - High avalanche danger in the upper canyon

Getting There

- **Access** - On Highway 26, drive east two miles beyond Government Camp. Take the Highway 35 exit (signed for Hood River). Follow Highway 35 for 4.2 miles to the White River Sno-park on the left. Two lots are available, use the second one. If you cross the river, you have driven too far.

- **Trailhead** - The obvious trail at the north end of the parking lot, often referred to as the Powerline Tour.
- **Map/Information** - Geo-Graphics - Mt. Hood Wilderness, Green Trails Mt. Hood # 462, USGS Mt. Hood South, Zig Zag Ranger District - 503-622-5741

White River Canyon offers a wide range of skiing options depending on snow conditions and your skiing ability. A large canyon resulting from a number of drainages above timberline, White River Canyon is a popular destination for touring and snowshoeing. The majority of the folks who visit the drainage are not in search of turns but are there to enjoy the spectacular views of Mt. Hood. Further and higher up the canyon several route options become available and fewer people are encountered. Near timberline, the canyon opens up and several ski options present themselves.

To access the upper canyon, begin on the trail at the north end of the parking lot. Follow this trail north along the west side of the canyon. The trail follows through the trees and up along the west ridge to timberline. From the timberline, follow the large moraine up the center of the canyon. The moraine is a safe approach to the upper canyon and has a steep east facing sidewall to descend or a more moderate descent following back down along the route of ascent. The east facing walls of the main canyon are extremely avalanche prone and the upper canyon walls commonly hold large cornices. The upper canyon should be avoided during unstable conditions and is best skied in spring. Always be wary of these slopes. As with many routes in *Oregon Descents*, spring consolidation opens a variety of terrain often unskiable during winter months.

Another option is to cross over to the east side of the canyon and follow the ridge up to the head of the canyon (6,000+ feet). This area offers a variety of small bowls and pitches to be skied down toward the main drainage. Again this area is prone to high avalanche danger and should always be evaluated before being skied. Skiing out the main drainage is not recommended because of exposure to avalanche prone slopes on the return.

Descending upper White River Canyon. June   *Photo Steve Boyer*

MT. HOOD - WY'EAST FACE

Wy'east follows the right hand skyline in this photograph. September

Route Information

- **Season** - April through June
- **Difficulty** - Expert
- **Total Skiing Vertical** - 3,000 ft.
- **Starting Elevation** - 5,950 ft.
- **Summit or Goal** - 11,239 ft.
- **Length** - 1 Day
- **Hazards** - High avalanche potential, glacier travel, crevasse exposure

Getting There

- **Access** - From Highway 26 in Government Camp, take the Timberline Mt. Road turn off and head toward Timberline Lodge. Access begins from Timberline Lodge parking lot. *Be sure to sign in at climber registration in the Wy' East Day Lodge (available 24 hours a day).*

PART ONE - MT HOOD

- ◆ **Trailhead** - South Side Climber's trail at the base of the Palmer Glacier, Palmer chair lift
- ◆ **Map/Information** - Geo-Graphics - Mt. Hood Wilderness, Green Trails Mt. Hood # 462, USGS Mt. Hood South, Zig Zag Ranger District - 503-622-5741

The Wy'east face is the beautiful east facing pitch above the White River and Heather Canyon drainages. With close to 1,000 vertical feet near 40 degrees and over 1,000 vertical feet closer to 30 degrees, Wy'east is a premier steep ski descent in Oregon. Not always skiable from the summit, the main face can be skied without reaching the summit. The top of the face is at about 10,700 feet and the remainder of the route, which follows the top of the Steel Cliffs, is more an exposed traverse than a skiable pitch. Wy'east is unique on Hood because, due to its eastern exposure, the face softens up hours before other aspects with similar elevations and is often protected from westerly winds that often sweep the south side. However, the eastern exposure does result in leeward slope loading. Lee slope loading combined with eastern sun exposure add up to high potential for avalanches. Be wary of Wy'east if the snow is overly soft or west winds and new snow have loaded the slope.

A couple of options exist for the ascent. The most common route of ascent is via Timberline Lodge and the start of the south side climbing route. Begin at Timberline as with the south side routes but between 7,000 and 8,000 feet begin to traverse eastward to cross the White River Glacier with the objective of gaining the far (east side) moraine of the White River Glacier. In April and May, climb as high as 9,000 or 9,200 and cross the White River Glacier just below the Steel Cliffs. Watch for rockfall below the Steel Cliffs (regardless of your traverse elevation) and be prepared to negotiate some large crevasses near 9,000 feet if on a high traverse. The Palmer chair can also be used to access the Wy'east route, but snow conditions need to be such that the face will remain firm for the ascent. See Palmer Chair access information at start of south side section for specifics on riding the chair. Once on the east side of the White River Glacier, you are on the Wy'east face. Ascend the face along climber's left until the pitch begins to mellow out and meets the summit ridge. This is the top of the Wy'east face. From here, you can either begin your descent or continue to the summit by traversing northeast above the Newton Clark Glacier and up toward the summit. The final climb to the summit is typically a short steep snow pitch nearing 50 degrees. The best place to begin a ski descent is from the top of the Wy'east face, not from the summit. The descent from 10,700 to 9,400 feet holds an average pitch near 40 degrees and is the highlight of the route.

A second option for ascent is to begin the climb from Mt. Hood Meadows and ascend the ridge between Heather and White River canyons. This route leads to an area on the Wy'east face just below a traverse from the south side. Although this route is longer (the start is about 1,000 feet lower), using Meadows for access allows for a longer, more continuous ski out and less crevasse field navigation to gain the route (not to mention a quieter parking lot scene, provided the ski area is closed for the season).

Looking down the Wy'east route from about 10,500 feet. May

MT. HOOD - NORTH SIDE ROUTES

The north side of Hood is the most inaccessible side of the mountain in the winter and early spring months. The Cloud Cap road # 3512 is often snow covered until beyond Memorial Day creating a several mile access hike. However, access should not deter a visit to the area. Often busy and 'overcrowded' on summer weekends, the north side in winter and early spring is well worth the access effort. Treeline skiing in midwinter and high alpine turns in spring are unmatched by other Hood locations. From the classic spring Snow Dome trip to the less travelled Ladd Glacier, the north side of Hood has a full range of terrain. Many of the routes on the north side can be strung together for several great days of skiing and a new appreciation for Mt. Hood.

Looking up the Snow dome at the north side of Hood. May

MT. HOOD - NORTH SIDE

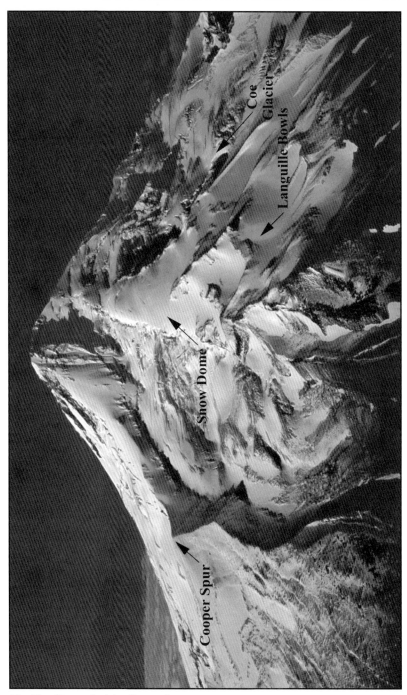

Mt. Hood's north side. September

PART ONE - MT HOOD

Summer turns in corn snow. June

MT. HOOD - BARRETT SPUR

Barret Spur from Elk Cove. June   Photo: *David Evans*

Route Information

- **Season** - April through July, winter option
- **Difficulty** - Advanced to Expert +
- **Total Skiing Vertical** - 2,000 + ft. (varies with season)
- **Starting** - 3600 ft.,
- **Summit Elevation** - 7,900 ft.
- **Length** - 1 day spring, 2 - 3 days in winter
- **Hazards** - Moderate to high avalanche potential in winter

Getting There

- **Access** - From Hood River, drive south toward Parkdale on Route 35. Thirteen miles out of Hood River, turn right onto Cooper Spur Road. (A general store is on the corner.) Follow signs for Parkdale and Cooper Spur. Drive 1.7 miles to a 4-way intersection and turn right towards Parkdale. Continue ½ mile to a railroad crossing and then make an immediate left onto Clear Creek Road. Drive Clear Creek for 2.7 miles and turn right onto Road 2840 (signed for Laurence Lake). Follow 2840 4.2 miles to a dirt road (# 650) signed for Elk Cove Trail and Pinnacle Ridge Trail. Turn left onto dirt road and follow two miles to Elk Cove Trail.

- **Trailhead** - Elk Cove Trail # 631
- **Map/Information** - Geo-Graphics - Mt. Hood Wilderness, Green Trails Mt. Hood # 462, Hood River Ranger District - 503-352-6002

Barrett Spur is a quiet area on the north side of Mt. Hood. While most routes on Hood give the sense of skiing on the mountain, Barrett Spur is unique because the feel is that of a distinct peak. Barrett Spur typically has skiable snow through early July and offers excellent vertical and pitch for the advanced skier. Winter access is also an option but be prepared to use a map and compass for access when the trail is snow covered. Furthermore, the access road may be snow covered during the winter and this adds distance to the approach. May and June are optimal months in average or above average snow years for a single day trip as described here.

Access Barrett via Elk Cove Trail # 631. Although trail # 631 is well established, it suffers from lack of trail maintenance. Be prepared for frequent blow down encountered along the way. A second access option, the Pinnacle Trail # 630, was in better condition as of 1997, but meets the ridge higher than trail # 631 and requires a climb back up about a thousand vertical feet to avoid missing almost a thousand vertical feet of good skiing. All information here is for access via trail # 631.

Trail # 631 climbs consistently from the trailhead to Elk Cove. Elk Cove sits 3.9 miles and 1,800 vertical feet into the hike and prior to June much of the trail can be skied using skins. A great place for a break, the Elk Cove is closed to overnight stays to limit environmental damage. Camping is only permitted when the cove area is snow covered. Otherwise, camping is possible on the ridge to the southwest or just below Elk Cove in the trees.

The climb from Elk Cove follows up the ridge just west of the Cove to a small bench at 7,200 feet (or if you access via trail # 630, cross the Timberline Trail and continue south gaining the ridge and continue to 7,200 feet). The bench is about 700 feet below the summit of the spur and is a good spot to begin skiing for those uncomfortable skiing the upper pitch. The spur has two summits. The near summit offers the most skiable lines. Skiing from the far summit offers 45 plus degree lines (expert +) down the east facing slopes of Barrett Spur. The near summit pitch is more skiable and offers several options for descent. Unmatched in length and consistency of pitch by any other low elevation skis on Mt. Hood, the lines from the near summit of the spur are what make Barrett a great destination. Exit via trail # 631 to return.

Barret Spur on USGS Mt. Hood North Map, elevation in meters

PART ONE - MT. HOOD

Turns in the spring corn from the summit of Barrett Spur. June

MT. HOOD - COE GLACIER

Looking west at Pulpit Rock on the upper Coe Glacier. May

Route Information

- **Season** - April through June
- **Difficulty** – Advanced
- **Total Vertical Skiing** - 2,000 ft., varies
- **Starting Elevation** - Varies
- **Summit or Goal** – 8,600 feet
- **Length** - 1 Day
- **Hazards** - Moderate avalanche danger, glacier travel

Getting There

- **Access** - Coming from the south (from Highway 26 & Government Camp), follow Highway 26 to Highway 35. Follow north on Highway 35 for 17 miles (just beyond the Polallie Picnic Area) and make a left turn on Road 3511 (signed Cooper Spur). Turn left again at the Tilly

Jane junction (signed for the Cooper Spur Ski Area) and follow the road as far as conditions will permit. Just beyond the Cooper Spur Ski Area is the official Sno-park for the Cooper Spur Ski Trail, but driving further on Cloud Cap Road 3512 is possible in spring. However, do not count on the Cloud Cap Road to be fully clear and graded until after Memorial Day.

Alternately, from Hood River, drive south on Highway 35 for 13 miles and turn right on Cooper Spur Road. (A general store is on the corner.) Follow the Cooper Spur Road another ten miles to the junction with Road 3511 (signed for Cooper Spur Ski area). Turn right and follow as far as conditions permit.

- **Trailhead** - Winter access is best from the Cloud Cap Ski Trail # 643, while spring and summer access are best from the Timberline Trail # 600 via the Cloud Cap Road or Cloud Cap parking area should the entire road be open.
- **Map/Information** - Geo-Graphics - Mt. Hood Wilderness; Green Trails Mt. Hood # 462; Hood River Ranger District 503-352-6002

The Coe Glacier route does not see a lot of skier traffic. The route traverses west from the Snow Dome and accesses the Coe Glacier just east of Pulpit Rock This route is a good choice for skiers who have accessed the Snow Dome before, who are up for some adventure and are looking to get to know the north side of Hood better. The ski follows the drainage to the west of the Langille snowfields. Although the terrain is only moderate in pitch, potential crevasse negotiation on the upper Coe warrants advanced abilities.

Access is virtually the same as for the Snow Dome so read the Snow Dome description if unfamiliar with the area. From the base of the Snow Dome, climb to about 8,600 feet and begin a west traverse toward Pulpit Rock. The trick is to drop through a notch in the ridge separating the Snow Dome from the Coe. Begin the traverse near 8,600 feet on the Snow Dome and prepare to adjust your route for the best line down to the Coe. Access to the Coe may require down climbing the ridge and a short section of crevasse negotiation depending on the snow conditions. Once on the Coe, explore to the west if conditions permit and or follow down the drainage. The Coe descends at a moderate (20-30 degrees) and consistent pitch for a couple thousand vertical feet. Skiing is often possible all the way to the Timberline Trail near 5,400 feet. Return by heading east via the Timberline Trail # 600.

Crevasse system on the north side of Mt. Hood. August

PART ONE - MT HOOD

MT. HOOD - COOPER SPUR

Looking up Cooper Spur Ridge from 8,500 feet. May Photo: David Evans

Route Information

- **Season** - December through July
- **Difficulty** - Intermediate to Advanced
- **Total Skiing Vertical** - 3,000 - 5,000 ft.
- **Starting Elevation** - 4,000 ft. - 5,700 ft.
- **Summit or Goal** - 8,600 ft. - 9,400 ft.
- **Length** - 1 Day +
- **Hazards** - Exposure and crevasse danger at high elevation, moderate to high avalanche danger above 8,600 ft.

Getting There

- **Access** - Coming from the south (from Highway 26 and Government Camp) follow Highway 26 to Highway 35. Follow north on Highway 35 for 17 miles (just beyond the Polallie Picnic Area) where you will see a left turn on Road 3511 (signed Cooper Spur). Follow left again at the Tilly Jane junction (signed for the Cooper Spur Ski Area) and follow the road as far as conditions will permit. Just beyond the Cooper Spur Ski Area is the official Sno-park for the Cooper Spur Ski Trail, but driving further on Cloud Cap Road 3512 is possible in spring. However, do not count on the Cloud Cap Road to be fully clear and graded until after Memorial Day.

Alternately, from Hood River, drive south on Highway 35 for 13 miles and turn right on Cooper Spur Road. (A general store is on the corner.) Follow the Cooper Spur Road another ten miles to the junction with Road 3511 (signed for Cooper Spur Ski area). Turn right and follow as far as conditions permit.

- **Trailhead** - Winter access is best through the Tilly Jane Campground via the Cooper Spur Ski Trail # 643. Spring and summer access is best from the Timberline Trail # 600 reached by Cloud Cap Road 3512 or from the Cloud Cap parking area should the entire road be open.
- **Map/Information** - Geo-Graphics - Mt. Hood Wilderness, Green Trails Mt. Hood # 462, Hood River Ranger District - 503-352-6002

The Cooper Spur area offers a wide variety of skiing options. Commonly skied in all seasons, the season dictates your options based on access and snow levels. Terrain ranges from treeline powder skiing in winter to high alpine corn snow come spring and summer. Climbing the Cooper Spur Ridge allows access to the Newton Clark Glacier bowls, the Elliot Glacier and the spur ridge itself. Winter and spring/summer yield two very different skiing experiences on Cooper Spur and two route descriptions follow; one is for winter and the other is for spring/summer.

WINTER

Winter season sees only limited traffic on the Cooper Spur Route. This route is a good choice on a winter day given new snow or when the weather allows travelling above treeline. Winter skiing generally means sticking to treeline where powder conditions can be found, but given good weather, venturing above timberline in winter is always rewarding regardless of the conditions. Winter access is best gained via the Cooper Spur Ski Trail # 643 just beyond the Cooper Spur Ski Area turn off. The trail goes up the north side of the Doe Creek drainage and skirts the edge of the Cooper Spur Ski Area. The trail climbs almost 2,000 vertical feet where it meets up with the Tilly Jane Campground and Shelter. (Check for shelter availability with the US Forest Service in Parkdale.)

The trail is well defined but in the right (or wrong) snow conditions can be a difficult (fast) descent. From the Tilly Jane campground and shelter area, continue climbing along the drainage and keep to climber's left of the drainage until near timberline. At timberline, (about 6,000 feet) head up the open drainage as far as conditions allow. The area above 7,000 feet is often windblown and hard pack in winter, while the lower elevations and treed areas can hold good snow in a variety of weather conditions. The broad flanks of the spur from about 8,200 feet on down can be great skiing any time of year. If the upper elevations do not offer good snow, try skiing in the trees and head north (left) to the Telephone Line Ski Trail. The Telephone Trail follows an old cut down through the trees to the northwest of the Cooper Spur ski trail and ends on Cloud Cap Road about 2.5 miles north of the Cooper Spur Sno-Park. Follow the road to return.

SPRING/SUMMER

Spring and summer bring a whole new set of options to ski in the Cooper Spur vicinity. Consolidated snow, longer days and shorter access all allow high alpine skiing. The Cooper Spur ridge allows access to both the Elliot and Newton Clark. The Elliot is a complex system of crevasses and ice fall but some good turns can be found. In contrast, the Newton Clark Glacier is an expansive glacier with several sweet moderate bowls. Access length is dictated by the snow coverage on Cloud Cap Road # 3512. Regardless, the skiing is well worth the trip. If the road is closed below 4,500 feet, be prepared for a long day or make it a two-day trip.

Drive, hike or ski whatever portion of Road 3512 necessary to reach the Cloud Cap parking area. From the Cloud Cap parking area/campground, follow the Timberline Trail southeast to timberline and meet the Elliot's east side moraine. Ascend Cooper Spur along the Elliot's east side moraine. The moraine eventually yields to the spur and the skiing options come into view. Alternately, access the spur via Tilly Jane is possible as described for the winter season access. Using the Tilly Jane option is probably the best choice if the road is closed below 4,500 feet.

Although the spur has been skied from the summit, the safest lines are from near 9,000 feet. The upper pitches from the summit follow a steep (45-50 degree) fall line down toward the Elliot Glacier headwall, and are for expert plus. From 9,000 feet, skiing the spur along the line of ascent is recommended. Alternatively, access the Newton Clark Glacier Bowls to the east or drop the steep north facing lines down toward the Elliot Glacier.

Skiing the spur along your line of ascent is the most straightforward option. Skiing the Newton Clark Glacier is an excellent option if the time is available to make the climb back to the spur. Many small bowls and fun lines are found in the Newton Clark drainage, allowing for several good runs. To avoid a lengthy exit hike, climb back up along the spur and exit via your ascent route.

The steep north facing lines down to the Elliot are best in early spring. Due to its exposure, the north facing snow is most skiable in the afternoon and makes for a good refuge when the Newton Clark Bowls become too soft. Be wary of crevasses running along the upper reaches of the pitch off the north side of the spur. The safest line is probably from the top of the spur itself at about 8,600 feet.

PART ONE - MT. HOOD

Cooper Spur from the north, Elliot Glacier in the center and the Snow Dome is just seen on the right. September

MT. HOOD - LADD GLACIER

Looking west across the upper Ladd Glacier. May

Route Information

- **Season** - April through June
- **Difficulty** - Advanced
- **Total Skiing Vertical** – 1,500 ft.
- **Starting Elevation** – 3,600 ft.
- **Summit or Goal** – 8,000 ft.
- **Length** – 1 Day
- **Hazards** - Potential crevasse negotiation

Getting There

- **Access -** From Hood River, drive south toward Parkdale on Route 35. Thirteen miles out of Hood River turn right onto Cooper Spur road. (A general store is on the corner.) Follow signs for Parkdale and Cooper Spur. Drive 1.7

miles to a 4-way intersection and turn right, this takes you into Parkdale. Continue ½ mile to a railroad crossing and then make an immediate left onto Clear Creek Road. Drive Clear Creek for 2.7 miles and turn right onto Road 2840 (signed for Laurence Lake). Follow 2840 4.2 miles to a dirt road (# 650) signed for Elk Cove Trail and Pinnacle Ridge Trail. Follow Road 650 3 miles to Pinnacle Ridge Trail.

- **Trailhead** – Pinnacle Ridge # 630
- **Map/Information** - Geo-Graphics - Mt. Hood Wilderness; Green Trails Mt. Hood # 462, Hood River Ranger District - 503-352-6002

The Ladd and Coe Glaciers make up one of the more complex crevasse systems on Hood, but the lower Ladd Glacier is relatively crevasse free and very skiable. With similar access as Barrett Spur, the Ladd Glacier lies just west of Barrett and is skiable from the saddle below Barrett Spur's summit. Best Skied in the early spring when the upper crevasse fields are well covered, the Ladd Glacier offers a less traveled option to the other spring skis on Hood's north side. Steeper, more accessible terrain can be found on Mt. Hood but for a change of venue or in combination with Barret Spur, the Ladd Glacier is great place to get some turns.

Access begins via the Pinnacle Ridge trail # 630. Follow the trail to timberline and gain the north facing shoulder of Barrett Spur. Follow the shoulder to a saddle (7,280 feet) below the steeper pitches leading to the summit of Barrett. From the saddle, drop west and onto the Ladd Glacier. Depending on snow coverage, the Ladd can be ascended further or the descent can begin here. Climbing from the saddle will put you in crevasse terrain, but, few if any crevasses should be encountered below the saddle. Descend as far as conditions permit and either link up with the Timberline Trail # 600 near Cairn Basin (about 5,800 feet) and follow the Trail east for one to one and a half miles back to the Pinnacle trail or climb back to the shoulder on Barrett to exit.

MT. HOOD - LANGILLE BOWLS

Looking up the Langille Bowls. July Photo: David Evans

Route Information

- **Season** - April through June
- **Difficulty** - Intermediate
- **Total Vertical Skiing** - 2,000 ft.
- **Starting Elevation** - Varies
- **Summit or Goal** - 8,000 ft.
- **Length** - 1 Day
- **Hazards** – Low avalanche potential

Getting There

- **Access** - Traveling from the south (Highway 26 and Government Camp) follow Highway 26 to Highway 35. Follow north on Highway 35 for 17 miles (just beyond the Polallie Picnic Area) and turn left on Road 3511 (signed Cooper Spur). Turn left again at the Tilly Jane junction (signed for the Cooper Spur Ski Area) and follow the road as far as conditions will permit. Just beyond the Cooper Spur Ski Area is the official Sno-park for the Cooper Spur Ski Trail, but driving further on Cloud Cap Road 3512 is possible in spring. However, do not count on the Cloud Cap Road to be fully clear and graded until after Memorial Day.

Alternately, from Hood River, drive south on Highway 35 for 13 miles and turn right on Cooper Spur Road. (A general store is on the corner.) Follow the Cooper Spur Road another ten miles to the junction with Road 3511 (signed for Cooper Spur Ski area). Turn right and follow as far as conditions permit.

- **Trailhead** - Spring and summer access are best from the Timberline Trail # 600 via the Cloud Cap Road or the Cloud Cap parking area should the entire road be open.
- **Map/Information** - Geo-Graphics - Mt. Hood Wilderness, Green Trails Mt. Hood # 462, Hood River Ranger District - 503-352-6002

The Langille Bowls are a great alternative to hiking the Snow Dome when snow conditions above 8,000 feet are poor, as a more moderate alternative or it can be used as a great addition to the Snow Dome descent. The bowls offer a range of descents including great intermediate skiing. The Langille glacier poses little or no crevasse hazard on a good snow year so the route is better for folks uncomfortable with the crevassed terrain found on either side of the Snow Dome. The bowls follow the fall line to the left (west) from the base of the Snow Dome and often take you all the way down to the timberline trail well into July. A few good steep lines are found on skier's left while the main bowl has a more moderate pitch.

Use the same access route as the Snow Dome or, from the Cloud Cap parking area, follow the Timberline Trail (#600) further west until you reach the Compass Creek drainages (the fifth and sixth drainages beyond the Cloud Cap trailhead). The Langille Bowl drainage has two distinct drainages, both of which offer access directly to the bowls. The Approach via the Timberline Trail is only a good option when the trail is no longer snow covered.

Looking west across the Langille Bowls. June *Photo: Jeff Schuh*

The upper pitch in the Langille Bowls. June *Photo: Heather Watkins*

MT. HOOD - SNOW DOME

Mt. Hood' from the north, the Snow Dome is the large snow field on the right. September

Route Information

- **Season** - April through September
- **Difficulty** - Intermediate + to Advanced
- **Total Skiing Vertical** - 1,000 - 3,000 ft.
- **Starting Elevation** - 5,800 ft.
- **Summit or Goal** - 9,100 ft.
- **Length** - 1 Day
- **Hazards** - Moderate avalanche danger, glacier travel

Getting There

- **Access** - Coming from the south (from Highway 26 and Government Camp) follow Highway 26 to Highway 35. Follow north on Highway 35 for 17 miles (just beyond the Polallie Picnic Area) where you will see a left turn on Road 3511 (signed Cooper Spur). Follow left again at the Tilly Jane junction (signed for the Cooper Spur Ski Area) and follow the road as far as conditions will permit. Just beyond the Cooper Spur Ski Area is the Sno-park for the Cooper Spur Ski Trail. Spring season typically allows you drive higher on Cloud Cap Road 3512.

Do not count on the Cloud Cap Road to be fully clear until after Memorial Day. Alternately, from Hood River, drive south on Highway 35 for 13 miles and turn right on Cooper Spur Road (general store on corner) and follow the Cooper Spur Road ten miles to the junction with Road 3511 (signed for Cooper Spur Ski Area). Turn right and follow as far as conditions permit.

- **Trailhead** - Winter access is best from the Cloud Cap Ski Trail # 643. Spring and summer access are best from the Timberline Trail # 600 via the Cloud Cap Road or Cloud Cap parking area should the entire road be open.
- **Map/Information** - Geo-Graphics - Mt. Hood Wilderness, Green Trails Mt. Hood # 462, Hood River Ranger District - 503-352-6002

The Snow Dome is the quintessential Mt. Hood north side ski route. Skiable virtually the entire year, the Snow Dome is a favorite destination to ski through late summer. Directly northwest of the Elliot glacier headwall, the upper reaches of the Snow Dome are just over 9,000 feet in elevation. Above the dome, technical glacier travel is required, and the standard route of ascent is called the Sunshine route (see *Oregon High*, by Jeff Thomas). Skiing from above the 9,000 foot level requires glacier travel and navigating the bergschrund among other hazards. The descent from below 9,000 feet, however, is straightforward and the start of what is often over a three thousand vertical foot descent, depending on the season. The Snow Dome itself is between 1,000 and 1,500 vertical feet in length depending on what is considered the base and a two options present themselves to continue the ski below 7,500 feet.

Spring access often includes a few miles hiking or skiing on the Cloud Cap Road 3512. This road typically opens by mid

June. Whether hiking or driving the road, follow it to Cloud Cap parking area Be sure to follow to the right when the road splits offering a left toward Tilly Jane. Once at the trailhead on the west side of the parking area, follow the Timberline Trail #600 northwest about a ¼ mile and cross over the drainage directly below the Elliot Glacier. The forest service maintains a seasonal bridge to cross this stream. Early season crossings are made possible by snow bridges. Once across the stream, follow the trail up the west side of the drainage until you roll over the ridge and reach a stand of trees. From this point, a small unmarked trail leads up to the left (west). The trail will lead you above treeline to the top of the moraine on the west side of the Elliot Glacier drainage. When the Timberline Trail is snow covered, this trail is difficult to locate. Be sure to gain the ridge directly across the creek upon the trees. The trail climbs steeply and the Snow Dome comes into view.

Follow the moraine to a the smaller drainage on your right. Several options are available for reaching the base of the Snow Dome from here. The least technical route is to cross the right hand drainage near its top and attain the next ridge to the right (often exposed rock by mid July) which leads directly to the snowfield at the base of the Snow Dome. Once at the base of the dome, simply head up the center to the 9,000 foot level. Climber's left yields to the Elliot crevasse fields and is commonly quite exposed by late summer. The rest of the Snow Dome remains a continuous snowfield nearly year round depending on the snow year. The base of the Snow Dome leads to additional skiing on the Langille and Coe Glaciers which, combined with the Dome, make for 2,000-3,000 foot runs. Camping at the base of the Dome allows access to all of the options and the area is well worth a couple days of skiing. Be prepared for a windy night should you decide to camp in the area. More information on skiing the Langille and Coe Glaciers is included in this chapter.

SNOW DOME

Looking down the Snow Dome with the nearby Elliot Glacier. August

Skiing below the Snow Dome. June

PART TWO
CENTRAL OREGON

Included in the Central Oregon region for the purposes of this guide are Mt. Jefferson, Three Sisters Wilderness and Diamond Peak. The weather and snow conditions found in the Mt. Jefferson region are similar to the conditions around Mt. Hood. Jefferson's access length and west slope snowpack make it most accessible in the spring. The Three Sisters Wilderness' more easterly location yields a more consistent and often lighter winter snowpack making the Three Sisters area a good choice for winter routes as well as spring. Diamond Peak's more southerly location makes it a target for strong southerly (warm) storms so winter conditions are not as consistent as those in the Sisters area, but the relatively short approach makes Diamond Peak a great early spring trip.

Central Oregon's Diamond Peak. March

MT. JEFFERSON
JEFFERSON PARK GLACIER

Jefferson Park Glacier from Jefferson Park. June

Route Information
- **Season** - May through July
- **Difficulty** - Advanced
- **Total Skiing Vertical** – 4,000 + ft.
- **Starting Elevation** – 4,100 ft.
- **Summit or Goal** – 9,600 ft.
- **Length** – 1 or 2 Days
- **Hazards** – Route finding in early spring, moderate avalanche potential, glacier travel

Getting There
- **Access** - Early spring and summer access to the Jefferson Park Glacier area are best from Route 22 (Santiam Pass road). Drive 10 miles east of Detroit, on Route 22 and turn left (east) on Whitewater Road # 2243. Be sure to stay on Road # 2243 (Road # 440 veers right at about

2700 feet but does not access the Whitewater drainage). Road 2243 is about 7.5 miles long but chances are it will be snow covered for some portion until June. When the road is snow covered try following the Sentinel Creek drainage (4,000 feet) about a mile before the trailhead.

- **Trailhead** - Use the Whitewater Trail # 3429 if accessible, otherwise follow the Sentinel Creek drainage from the sharp left in the road at 4,000 feet.
- **Map/Information** - Geo-Graphics - Mt. Jefferson Wilderness, Green Trails Mt. Jefferson # 557, Detroit Ranger Station - 541-854-3366.

At 10,497 feet, Mt. Jefferson is the second highest peak in Oregon. Although the summit pinnacle of Jefferson is not skiable, skiing is excellent several places on the mountain. The drawback to Mt. Jefferson is access length. Long access makes for a long day, but keeps climber numbers down. This gives Jefferson a nice removed feeling. The less glaciated south side climbing route offers moderate skiing but requires very long access at the time of year when the route is still snow covered. The Jefferson Park Glacier on the north side has shorter access (4.5 miles), provides an excellent ski mountaineering objective and, based on its north aspect, holds snow well into June and July.

Access to the glacier is gained via the north ridge dividing the Jefferson Park Glacier from the Whitewater Glacier. The most straightforward descent drops onto the Jefferson Park Glacier from a notch in the north ridge at about 9,600 feet. The route winds down along the east side of the glacier and crosses crevassed terrain

If the road is clear of snow, begin at the Whitewater Trailhead # 3429. If not, follow the Sentinel Creek drainage from Road 2243 about a mile before the trailhead (4,000 feet). The drainage meets the main trail just as it gains the lower Sentinel Ridge between 4,800 and 4,900 feet. Jefferson Park has good snow conditions into June and the access is easiest when the snow coverage is at or above 5,000 feet. The trail is difficult to follow when snow coverage is below 5,000 feet and requires map and compass work to avoid wasted time.

Once the ridge is gained (the trail is marked with a sign indicating the Whitewater / Triangulation Peak trail junction), follow the ridge eastward, gain elevation slowly to about 5,500 feet and traversing above the large Whitewater drainage. The exposure above Whitewater drainage is steep and the trail commonly has large drifts making travel difficult. The trail eventually crosses the upper reaches of Whitewater Creek and enters Jefferson Park. A bridge crosses the creek but a wall of snow often blocks the far side.

From Jefferson Park, head southeast toward the center of the Jefferson Park Glacier. The drainage yields to a moraine heading up the middle of the glacier. Follow the moraine to about 7,800 feet and traverse east (left) and gain the north ridge or follow up the eastern edge of the glacier. Following the ridge is recommended if it is snow covered, but loose rock can make the ridge frustrating when clear of snow. Initially, following the east side of the glacier is straightforward but becomes steep and exposed to crevasses as it nears 9,000 feet. Either way, climb to the notch in the north ridge around 9,600 feet. Depending on crevasse exposure, traverse out below the pinnacles and descend or ski the line directly off the notch. Climbing and skiing the Jefferson Park Glacier requires crampons, ice axe and the ability to route find on the access as well as on the glacier.

If the Jefferson Park Glacier appears too crevassed or time is short, consider the Russell Glacier just west of the Jefferson Park Glacier. The Russell is close to a thousand feet lower and offers more moderate terrain than the Jefferson. The initial access is the same as for Jefferson Park but once across Whitewater Creek, follow the first drainage to the right (south) or from the moraine on Jefferson Park, traverse west and drop into the Russell Glacier drainage from near 7,700 feet. See *Oregon High*, by Jeff Thomas for more details on Mt. Jefferson climbing routes. Exit via your access route.

PART TWO - CENTRAL OREGON

Tracks dropping into Jefferson Park, above which is the Jefferson Park Glacier. June

JEFFERSON PARK
PARK BUTTE/PARK RIDGE

Jefferson Park and the surrounding Park Butte / Park Ridge area from the south. June

Route Information
- **Season** - April through June
- **Difficulty** - Advanced
- **Total Skiing Vertical** – 2,000 - 3,000 ft.
- **Starting Elevation** – 4,100 ft.
- **Summit or Goal** – 7,000 ft.
- **Length** – 1 - 2 Days
- **Hazards** – Route finding in early spring, moderate avalanche potential

Getting There
- **Access -** Early spring and summer access to the Jefferson Park Glacier area are best from Route 22 (Santiam Pass road). Drive east on Route 22 for 10 miles beyond Detroit, and turn left (east) on Whitewater Road # 2243. Be sure to stay on Road # 2243 (Forest Service Road #

440 veers right at about 2700 feet but does not access the Whitewater drainage). Road 2243 is about 7.5 miles long but some portion will be snow covered until June. When the road is snow covered, try following the Sentinel Creek drainage (4,000 feet) about a mile before the trailhead.

- **Trailhead** - Use the Whitewater Trail #3429 if accessible; otherwise follow the Sentinel Creek drainage from the sharp left in the road at 4,000 feet.
- **Map/Information** - Geo-Graphics - Mt. Jefferson Wilderness, Green Trails Mt. Jefferson # 557, Detroit Ranger Station - 541-854-3366

An alternative to skiing the Jefferson Park Glacier is to ski Park Butte and Park Ridge directly north of Jefferson Park. Although the summit and ridge elevations are only about 7,000 feet, the area holds snow through May in good snow years. The ridge and butte offer a variety of terrain and compliment skiing the Jefferson Park Glacier on a multi-day trip. The Park Butte area also has fine intermediate ski terrain.

Access Jefferson Park according to the directions for skiing the Jefferson Park Glacier. From Jefferson Park, the ridge and butte come into view to the north. Park Butte is accessible from Park Ridge or from the Russell Lake drainage. The ridge offers more varied terrain but both the Ridge and the Butte are worthy of a couple of laps. Chances are the lakes in Jefferson Park will be snow covered but the area offers a wide variety of camping options if you choose to spend the night. Early spring is a great time to enjoy this area which sees heavy traffic come summer after the snow melts.

THREE SISTERS WILDERNESS

Unique to Oregon, the Three Sisters Wilderness is a classic alpine basin with several prominent high peaks. Included in the area for the purposes of this guide are Broken Top, Middle Sister, North Sister, South Sister and a couple of smaller peaks. Although heavily used during the summer months, many areas in the Three Sisters Wilderness are difficult to access in the winter and early spring due to long approach routes. Several of the routes in the area lose their snow by midsummer so spring is by far the best time to ski despite the added approach distance. West side approaches are made easier when the Cascade Lakes Highway opens (typically near Memorial Day) but the area can be accessed before the road opens. The long access distance adds a challenge but makes for a great backcountry trip. In winter and early spring, the Cascade Lakes Highway is very busy with snowmobiles. The machines are restricted to the nonwilderness areas but are inevitably encountered somewhere along the way. To minimize encounters, begin access from the Mt. Bachelor Nordic Center rather than from the Dutchman Flat Sno-park and stick to the marked ski routes rather than the snow covered roads for access.

Several days can be spent climbing, skiing and traversing a variety of the peaks in the area and such a trip makes for an excellent winter or spring adventure. As with most Cascade routes, the snow above 8,000 - 9,000 feet in winter is often windblown hardpack while the lower elevations hold better snow conditions midwinter. Spring is another story. Skiable snow can be found from the summit of South Sister at 10,300 feet all the way down to near 5,000 feet. The Sisters Wilderness offers stunning views and the combined terrain is unmatched in the Southern Cascade region.

PART TWO - CENTRAL OREGON

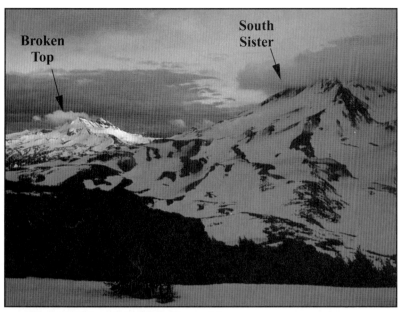

Looking south from the Middle Sister. May

Looking west from the Pole Creek approach trail. May

BROKEN TOP
CRATER BOWL / SW RIDGE

Broken Top from the southwest. January

Route Information

- **Season** - December through June
- **Difficulty** - Intermediate + to Expert
- **Total Skiing Vertical** - 2,000 ft., varies
- **Starting Elevation** - 6,000 ft.
- **Summit or Goal** - Varies
- **Length** - 1 Day +
- **Hazards** - Moderate to high avalanche potential

Getting There

- **Access** - From downtown Bend, follow the signs for Mt. Bachelor and the Cascade Lakes Highway (Road 46). In winter, follow Road 46 for 21 miles to the Mt. Bachelor parking lot. Winter access begins from either

PART TWO - CENTRAL OREGON

the Mt. Bachelor Nordic lot or the Dutchman Flat Sno-park. Dutchman Flat is often packed with snowmobilers (the Bachelor lot is quieter). In other seasons, when the Cascade Lakes Highway is open, access can begin from the Todd Lake road (1.5 miles beyond Dutchman Flat sno-park).

- **Trailhead** - Winter access uses Dutchman Flat or from the Bachelor Nordic Center follow the Common Corridor to the Dutchman Flat area
- **Map/Information** - Geo-Graphics - Three Sisters Wilderness Map, Bend Ranger District - 541-388-5664

Broken Top is the most accessible peak in the Three Sisters Wilderness during the winter months. The winter also brings many snowmobiles to the area. To avoid weekend skidoo, crowds begin your trip from the Mt. Bachelor Nordic Center. Overnight parking is permitted and the Nordic Center provides a 'Common Corridor' to access the Dutchman Flat and Todd Lake areas.

Although no lines are skiable from the actual rocky summit, several ski options exist on Broken Top. The terrain ranges from skiing the northwest and southwest ridgelines of Broken Top to skiing lines in the crater. The ridgelines are moderate while the crater lines offer steep (near 50 degree) terrain. While Broken Top offers a range of ski options, the access can be difficult. Often requiring creative route finding, the approach to Broken Top is not for the inexperienced skier. Map skills aid in access and in the event of poor weather solid map skills are a necessity.

Whether beginning from Mt. Bachelor Nordic Lot, Dutchman Flat or Todd Lake Road, follow the marked cross-country ski routes to the Todd Lake picnic area (from the Nordic Center follow the Lower Todd Meadow loop, from Dutchman flat follow the Water Tower/Upper Todd Meadow trail). The route beyond Todd Lake is less defined. In winter, follow a mix of snowmobile and ski trails to the Crater Creek drainage and continue northwest up the drainage toward the south shoulder of Broken Top. Alternatively in winter, break trail heading north from Todd Lake on a course for the south side of Broken Top. Breaking trail from Todd Lake requires creative route finding but also allows for some turns to be had along the way. If the choice is made to travel directly from Todd Lake, be prepared for a potentially difficult stream crossing on Soda Creek. The best way to minimize the difficulty of crossing is to cross as far east as possible. In the spring, when access to the Todd Lake area is possible via the road, pick up the upper Todd Trail #34 and follow it north to connect with the Crater Creek drainage.

Near 7,000 feet around the open slopes below the south side of Broken Top several options exist. To ski the crater lines you simply follow up into the center of the crater. The descent options are from the various saddles on either side of the true summit of Broken Top. The more south facing crater wall (climber's right side) offers a 30 to 40 degree pitch, while the more east facing (climber's left) side offers steeper 40 to 50 degree lines. Be prepared to evaluate avalanche hazard as well as encounter cornices on the various saddles. Other options are to ascend the ramp like south shoulder of Broken Top and ski either the couloirs leading down towards the crater or the west facing pitch off the opposite side. The west facing pitch is probably best skied in the spring due to its west aspect and wind swept nature in the winter.

Still another option is to traverse to the northwest from the south shoulder in order to gain the northwest ridge of Broken Top. The Northwest ridge offers the most moderate lines of the various options and can be skied on the north or south facing aspects. The Northwest Ridge is the longest approach from the Todd Lake area and requires a long day. An alternative to the Todd Lake access is to enter via the north side and Green Lakes. Due to road closures, access from the north side is best planned during a longer trip in combination with South Sister or Tam McArthur Rim trip. Any ski to Broken Top should include crampons and an ice axe to help with travel on hardpack windblown slopes.

In addition to the routes described here, the area just southeast of Broken Top offers several shorter trips. Both Moon

Mountain and Ball Butte have skiable lines and shorter access than Broken Top. Although nearer to skidoo traffic, Moon Mountain holds good winter snow and Ball Butte, higher and more exposed, is also worthy of a trip.

Broken Top from the North. May

MIDDLE SISTER SOUTHEAST RIDGE

Middle Sister's east, the Southeast Ridge follows the left skyline. May

Route Information
- **Season** - April through June
- **Difficulty** - Expert
- **Total Skiing Vertical** - 3,000 - 4,000 ft.
- **Starting Elevation** - 5,100 ft.
- **Summit or Goal** - 10,053 ft.
- **Length** - Multi-day
- **Hazards** - Moderate avalanche, glacier travel

Getting There
- **Access** - From Sisters, head west on Route 242 one mile to the intersection with Forest Service Road 15 (Pole Creek Rd.). Turn left on Pole Creek Road and follow signs to Pole Creek Campground, about 10 miles.

- **Trailhead** - Pole Creek Trail # 96D
- **Map/Information** - Geo-Graphics - Three Sisters Wilderness Map, Sisters Ranger District - 541-388-5664

Although the Middle Sister has the lowest elevation of the Three Sisters, the Southeast Ridge is one of the longer, steeper skiable ridgelines in Oregon. The setting and exposure of the route make for a classic summit ski descent. Balanced between the steep east face and the more moderate southwest face, the southeast ridge holds a 30 - 40 degree pitch for nearly three thousand feet.

The hike in is along the Pole Creek Trail (96D) to Soap Creek at 5,700 feet. A bridge makes for easy crossing but the trail beyond this point is often snow covered and, thus, difficult to follow. On the far side of the creek is a trail sign marking Green Lakes to the south and Chambers Lake to the west. Follow west towards Chambers Lake. If the trail is snow covered, keep an eye out for old blazes marking the trail and keep a southwest heading in-line with the trail on the map. The trail goes in the direction of the Squaw Creek drainage. Once near the drainage, follow the north (right) side of the drainage up hill. The Sisters soon come into view and maintaining a line toward the saddle between the Middle and North Sisters sets up a good approach to any route in the area.

The Southeast Ridge is the southern (left side) skyline of the Middle Sister. The route of ascent follows the far side of the ridge. You can choose to cross the Diller Glacier between 7,500 and 8,500 feet. A bench on the south ridge at 8,000 feet makes a great camp site. Use caution in traversing the Diller Glacier, the crevasses run all the way to the ridge and may require a navigation for both ascent and descent depending on the snowpack. Once on the ridge, simply follow the ridgeline to the summit. The skiable snowfields include the ridgeline and bowls with a more southwestern exposure. The ridge holds the steepest, most sustained fall line but the pitches wrapping west allow you to drop down into the west side drainages for more adventure. Crampons are often necessary and skins can ease the approach hike.

Crevasses on the Diller Glacier running near the Southeast Ridge on Middle Sister, Broken Top in the distance. May

MIDDLE SISTER
PROUTY PINNACLE / NORTH RIDGE

Middle Sister from the east. May

Route Information

- **Season** - April through June
- **Difficulty** - Advanced
- **Total Skiing Vertical** - 3,000 - 4,000 ft.
- **Starting Elevation** - 5,100 ft.
- **Summit or Goal** – 9,312 - 10,053 ft.
- **Length** – 1-2 days
- **Hazards** - Moderate avalanche, glacier travel

Getting There

- **Access** - From Sisters, head west on Route 242 one mile to the intersection with Forest Service Road 15 (Pole Creek Road). Turn left on Pole Creek Road and follow signs to Pole Creek Campground, about 10 miles.

MIDDLE SISTER - PROUTY PINNACLE

- **Trailhead** - Pole Creek Trail # 96D
- **Map/Information** - Geo-Graphics - Three Sisters Wilderness Map, Sisters Ranger District - 541-388-5664

The Prouty Pinnacle descent is a more moderate alternative to the Southeast Ridge ski. Although the pinnacle descent does not require reaching the summit, the route is well worth accessing and can be combined with the North Ridge for a descent from the summit of the Middle Sister. The upper reaches of the North Ridge often feature a short, steep (near 45 degrees) section, depending on the snowpack. Aside from this upper pitch, the descent averages closer to 30 degrees. The lower reaches from the saddle with Prouty Pinnacle hold a variety of small bowls that lead down to timberline. Regardless of whether reaching the summit is planned, glacier travel is required for the ascent to the saddle.

The approach hike is the same as for the Southeast Ridge, so refer to this route description for the Southeast Ridge. Once the Middle and North Sisters come into view, head for the saddle between them. Prouty Pinnacle is the high point in the saddle between the two peaks. The route ascends the east side of the Middle Sister crosses the Hayden Glacier between 8,000 and 9,000 feet and aims for the Saddle just left of Prouty Pinnacle. The ski terrain from the saddle down is moderate in pitch but does involve crossing the Hayden Glacier so caution is advised. The lower reaches provide a few short steep pitches depending on route selection. The lower area is a great spot to make multiple laps while camped in the near treeline.

To summit via this route, gain the saddle just left of Prouty Pinnacle and ascend the North Ridge. Folks interested in reaching the summit need to be prepared for steep icy conditions on the North Ridge. Crampons, ice axes and protection for this section may be necessary.

NORTH SISTER SOUTHEAST RIDGE

Looking up the Southeast Ridge of North Sister, skiing is found on both sides of the ridge. May

Route Information
- **Season** - April through June
- **Difficulty** – Intermediate + to Advanced
- **Total Skiing Vertical** - 1,000 - 2,000 ft.
- **Starting Elevation** - 5,100 ft.
- **Summit or Goal** – 8,800- 9,400 ft.
- **Length** – 1-2 days
- **Hazards** - Moderate avalanche

Getting There
- **Access** - From Sisters, head west on Route 242 one mile to the intersection with Forest Service Road 15 (Pole Creek Rd.). Turn left on Pole Creek Road and follow signs to Pole Creek Campground, about 10 miles.

NORTH SISTER

- **Trailhead** - Pole Creek Trail 96D
- **Map/Information** - Geo-Graphics - Three Sisters Wilderness Map, Sisters Ranger District - 541-388-5664

Although the North Sister does not offer the long continuous summit descents like those of the Middle and South Sisters, the North Sister has a few ridges worth the trip if time permits. A ski from the summit of the North Sister involves sustained, narrow, steep terrain not appealing to most skiers. However, the Southeast Ridge and South Face below the pinnacles are both skiable near or below 9,400 feet. The area loses its snow early in the spring due to southern exposure and is best visited in conjunction with a trip to the Middle Sister rather than a destination on its own. The South Face nears 45 degrees while the ridge holds more moderate terrain.

The access hike is the same as for the Middle Sister routes so refer to the Southeast Ridge route description. Once in the basin between the Middle and North Sister, the Southeast Ridge is the large ramp leading up the east (right) side of the basin between the Middle and North Sister. Descents can de made from short sections off any point on the ridge or for more vertical continue up the ridge to ski the South Face. Return via Pole Creek or start a multiple day trip by warming up here.

SOUTH SISTER SOUTH SIDE

South Sister from the south. January   *Photo: Roger Alfred*

Route Information
- **Season** - December through July
- **Difficulty** - Intermediate + to Advanced in winter
- **Total Skiing Vertical** - 3,500 ft.
- **Starting Elevation** - 5,500 ft.
- **Summit or Goal** -10,358 ft.
- **Length** – 1-2 day spring and summer, 2-3 days in winter
- **Hazards** - Moderate avalanche potential, winter route finding

Getting There
- **Access** - From downtown Bend, follow the signs for Mt. Bachelor and the Cascade Lakes Highway (Road 46). In winter, follow Road 46 twenty-one miles to the Mt. Bachelor parking lot. Winter access begins at the Bachelor Nordic Center. The opening of the Cascade

Lakes Highway beyond the Bachelor lot facilitates spring and summer access. Whether the road is hiked or driven, follow it about 5 ½ miles past Mt. Bachelor to Devil's Lake Campground.

- **Trailhead -** Devils Lake Campground / South side climbing route
- **Map/Information** - Geo-Graphics - Three Sisters Wilderness Map, Bend Ranger District - 541-388-5664

The South Sister is a classic Cascade descent. One of the top peaks for continuous vertical skiing, South Sister presents little in the way of technical difficulties for the ascent and is a spring ritual for many skiers. When the highway is closed the approach is about five miles longer and a two day trip is recommended. Aside from snowmobile traffic on the road itself, few other people will be encountered in the area during a winter or early spring trip.

Follow the Cascade Lakes Highway to the Devil's Lake campground and begin the South Side Climber's route from the north side of the road. If snow still covers the trail at the road, follow the Hell Creek drainage north (almost directly opposite the small plowed parking area and Devils Lake Camp Road). The trail goes north up the drainage between Kaleetan Butte and Devils Hill. The drainage is narrow at times so stay on the trail or in the drainage to avoid steeper sections found off the trail. Near timberline (6,700 feet), the trail intersects the Moraine Lake trail. Continue north on the climber's trail staying to the right (east) of Little Broken Top (an obvious rock outcropping resembling Broken Top) as you enter an open plateau. A large lava flow is also visible on the left (west). Continue climbing north along one of the many ridges or obvious lines to the summit. Be cautious to stay left (west) of the Lewis Glacier near 8,900 feet and continue on to the summit.

Two good descent routes can be followed. One is to follow a good fall-line down along the ascent route. Alternatively a more southeast aspect can be skied toward Green Lakes. The Green Lakes route requires a longer ski out once off the mountain, but is a less traveled descent and sets up a descent of the Northwest Ridge and west facing bowl on Broken Top should multi day trip be possible. The Green Lakes descent can also be combined with a traverse near 7,600 feet to return to the original ascent route and avoiding the longer slog out.

The South Sister, north side. May

DIAMOND PEAK
WEST SIDE

Diamond Peak from the west. March

Route Information
- **Season** - February through June
- **Difficulty** - Advanced
- **Total Skiing Vertical** - 2,000 ft.
- **Starting Elevation** - 4,000 -5,000 ft.
- **Summit or Goal** - 8,744 ft.
- **Length** - 2-3 Days
- **Hazards** - Moderate to high avalanche potential

Getting There
- **Access** - From Oakridge, drive south of town on Highway 58 about a mile and turn right on Forest Service Road 21 (signed Rigdon Road). Road 21 turns right a half mile from Highway 58 and follows south

along the west side of Hills Creek Reservoir. Continue on Road 21 approximately 30 miles to spur Road 2149. Turn left on Road 2149 and follow as far as conditions permit or to the Corrigan Lake Trail # 3654 (approximately 5 miles).
- **Trailhead** - Corrigan Lake Trail # 3654
- **Map/Information** - Imus Geographics - Diamond Peak Wilderness, USFS Willamette National Forest map is useful for driving portion. Rigdon Ranger District - 541-782-2283

Located southeast of Oakridge, Oregon, Diamond Peak stands at 8,744 feet. A broad peak with several sub-summits, it offers many skiable bowls including moderate lines directly off the summit. Best skied in winter or early spring, Diamond Peak is not a heavily visited area during these seasons and is great for a multi-day trip. Although possible as a two day trip, enough skiable terrain is available for several days of skiing. The most accessible slopes are on the west side of the main peak but several tempting bowls are on the east and north sides as well.

A reliable winter and spring access point is the Corrigan Lake Trailhead on Road 2149. A map and compass are essential for the approach when the trail is snow covered. The trees are thick and several small drainages can lead one astray. Use Corrigan Lake as land mark to stay on course when the area is snow covered. The climb is less than four thousand vertical feet from the trailhead but the gain takes place over several miles often made even longer by snow on Road 2149. If driving to about 3,500 or 4,000 feet is possible, a two to three day trip is recommended. Many skiable routes exist so the more time, the better.

Beginning from the Corrigan Lake Trail (approximately 5,000 feet), head northeast through thick trees and up the ridge until it levels out near the lake. From the lake, continue northeast and work up toward the southwest facing ridge that rises above the lake. Then, staying along the northwest side of the ridge work your way up through the drainage to gain the ridge and follow it to timberline. The ridge will put you west of the summit and setup to ascend along the southwest facing ridgeline. Camping is possible around 7,200 feet on a small saddle in the ridge near timberline. From the ridge, descents can be chosen from among the many bowls that are present or make a summit attempt. Use the ridge as a route of ascent or climb the next ridge to the east for a more direct and steeper route. As with many of the Cascade volcanoes, the upper reaches of the peak can be icy and wind blown but under good conditions Diamond Peak is skiable from the summit. The large saddle at about 8,500 feet just west of the summit allows access to the northeast facing bowls that are a destination in their own right.

Many of the bowls on Diamond Peak are exposed to avalanches and all slopes should be evaluated prior to skiing or climbing. The area is remote and in the event of an emergency the trailhead is a long way out, so ski smart. Crampons will aid in an early morning ascent above treeline when the snow is hard and the ascent along the southwest ridge has some steep traverses for which crampons are needed.

As of 1997, Diamond Peak Espresso in Oakridge is a source of good coffee and the owner may be helpful with road and trail conditions. Stop by for your fix and some local beta.

East side bowls on Diamond Peak. March

Climbing the West Ridge of Diamond Peak. March

PART THREE
SOUTHERN OREGON

Reaching as far south as Northern California, the Southern Cascades have several excellent ski destinations. Just as their northern counterparts, the Southern Cascades receive heavy winter snows and offer relatively easy access. Although the snowpack may not remain as long into the spring as on more northerly peaks, excellent spring skiing conditions can be found in the Southern Cascades. Rising above Diamond Lake is Mt. Bailey. Near 8,300 feet, the summit of Mt. Bailey offers several descent options. Sky Lakes Wilderness east of Medford, Oregon contains Mt. McLoughlin, a symmetrical volcano rising to over 9,000 feet. McLoughlin offers a straightforward approach and great terrain for the intermediate and advanced skier. Further south at over 14,000 feet, Mt. Shasta is recognized throughout the West as a skier's mountain and serves as a grand sentinel on the Cascades southern end.

In addition to the routes described here, Southern Oregon has other areas worthy of a visit such as Crater Lake's Mt. Scott and the Mt. Thielsen Wilderness.

Mt. McLoughlin, looking down the Southeast Side. May

PART THREE - SOUTHERN OREGON

MT. BAILEY
EAST FACE / WEST FACE

Mt. Bailey from the east side of Diamond Lake. October

Route Information

- **Season** - January through May
- **Difficulty** - Advanced to Expert
- **Total Skiing Vertical** - 2,000 - 3,000 ft.
- **Starting Elevation** - 5,250 ft.
- **Summit or Goal** - 8,360 ft.
- **Length** - 1 Day
- **Hazards** - High avalanche

Getting There

- **Access** - From Highway 97 on the east side, take Route 138 west for 18 miles. Turn left (west) on Route 230 and follow the signs for Diamond Lake's South Shore/Broken Arrow Camp. Take the next right onto Road 6592 and again follow signs for South Shore and Broken

MT. BAILEY

Arrow Camp. Follow 6592 for 0.7 of a mile and turn left. Continue to follow signs for South Shore and Broken Arrow Camp. Follow this road for 1.7 miles to an unmarked left turn onto dirt road # 300. The trailhead is exactly 0.4 miles down this road on the right. During winter months and early spring, park on the South Shore Road where it is closed. In winter this will essentially be at the turn off from Road 6592, while spring will allow driving further depending on snowpack.

- **Trailhead -** Mt. Bailey Trail # 1451
- **Map/Information -** USFS Diamond Lake map, Umpqua National Forest Diamond Lake Ranger District, 541-498-2531. *Many of the maps for this area are out of date, be sure to have the Umpqua National Forest map in addition to the topographic map to aid in finding all necessary roads.*

Mt. Bailey sits on the west side of Diamond Lake about 30 miles north of Crater Lake in Southern Oregon. With grand views ranging from Mt. Shasta to Mt. Jefferson, Bailey's position on Diamond Lake offers a beautiful setting to ski winter or spring. The upper east side of Bailey approaches 50 degrees in places, and much of the remaining terrain is at least 30 degrees.

Sounds too good to be true? Well, a few details be kept in mind. Number one, you will not be alone in the Diamond Lake area in the winter months. Largely developed as a snowmobiler destination, a snowcat ski operation also runs on Mt. Bailey. Second, the East Face, the most accessible aspect via ski or foot, is inherently avalanche prone due to its generally lee aspect and angle of pitch. A large slide path near 30 years old marks the East Face. Skiing the face is a serious undertaking and requires careful slope evaluation. In addition to the natural avalanche potential on many aspects of Mt. Bailey, the snowcat company does their own avalanche control work and will not be looking out for you.

The final detail to consider before skiing Bailey is the

PART THREE - SOUTHERN OREGON

approach. Nearly seven miles in winter, the approach is committing. The first three miles are mostly flat while the climb on the Mt. Bailey trail is about 4.5 miles and 3,000 vertical feet.

This said, Bailey remains a great ski descent and waiting until late spring helps solve many of the problems such as approach length, snowmobile traffic and snow stability. So, in the least Bailey is an accessible spring descent. Winter trips require strong skiing and snow evaluation skills as well as the need to avoid any snowcat traffic. Many aspects of Bailey are skiable but unless several days are spent to accommodate returning to your vehicle, the East Face and Southeast Ridge are really the most practical and convenient from the access route described here.

The best approach winter or spring is via Mt. Bailey Trail 1451. Following up the southeast ridge, Trail 1451 is well blazed with cross-country ski trail markers (blue diamonds) from 5,250 feet to about 6,800 feet and is closed to motorized traffic. The trail climbs moderately for about a mile, levels out until it reaches about 6,100 feet and then climbs consistently to treeline. The ski trail blazes end near 6,800 feet at which point a short traverse to the left (south) allows climbing more directly along the ridge and then gains timberline. From timberline, follow the ridge northwest. Near 7,600 you may need to traverse around the south side to avoid steep, potentially rocky terrain. A large natural bowl on the slope here is good for some entertaining runs. The best approach to the summit continues the traverse around the south shoulder toward the west face and heads for the summit from the more moderate west side.

Once the summit ridge is gained, a variety of terrain is accessible. Depending on snow conditions and snowcat traffic, the best aspects to ski are the East Face, the West Face, the Southeast Ridge(ridge used for access) or the East Ridge(ridge on the far side of the East Face). The West Face is often wind blown but offers a consistent 30 degree pitch. Skiing the West Face requires traversing or climbing to exit via the ascent route.

The East Face is the bowl of choice given stable snow conditions, while the East Ridge is a more moderate option than the Face. Either route will require a short traverse south after the descent in order to regain the approach trail. Traverse near 6,500 feet for a return to the access route without terrible difficulty.

Looking south along the summit ridge and East Face of Mt. Bailey. October

PART THREE - SOUTHERN OREGON

MT. MCLOUGHLIN SOUTHEAST / NORTHEAST SIDES

Looking up the east ridge of Mt. McLoughlin. May

Route Information

- ◆ **Season** - January through May
- ◆ **Difficulty** - Intermediate to Advanced
- ◆ **Total Skiing Vertical** - 2,000 - 4,000 ft.
- ◆ **Starting Elevation** - 5,500 ft.
- ◆ **Summit or Goal** - 9,495 ft.
- ◆ **Length** - 1 Day
- ◆ **Hazards** - Moderate to high avalanche danger

Getting There

- ◆ **Access** - Head north on Highway 62 from Medford, Oregon about 3 miles to the junction with Highway 140. Head east on 140 for 30 miles and turn left on Forest Service Road 3650 (which is marked as a sno-park and signed Summit Trail). Follow Road 3650 to the Mt.

MT. MCLOUGHLIN

McLoughlin Trailhead (a well marked parking area at junction with Road 3661). Should 3650 be blocked by snow, try following Highway 140 about 2.5 miles further to Road 3661. If both are blocked by snow, park at 3650 and ski the remainder.

- **Trailhead** - Mt. McLoughlin Trail # 3716
- **Map/Information** - USFS Sky Lakes Wilderness topographic map, Rogue River National Forest map, Rogue River National Forest District Ranger - 541-865-2700 or Winema National Forest District Ranger 541-885-3400

Standing at 9,495 feet, Mt. McLoughlin is the highest point in the Sky Lakes Wilderness Area located about forty miles east of Medford, Oregon. The beauty of McLoughlin is that beginner climbers with intermediate or better skiing skills can get a true summit ski and nearly 4,000 vertical feet of skiing. The Southern Oregon snowpack does not last as long as Northern Oregon coverage and, although a good snow year may see skiing through mid June, the best snow will be found March through May. A bit out of the way for folks in northern Oregon, McLoughlin is well worth the trip. Mt. McLoughlin is a symmetric volcano with a variety of descent lines directly off its summit. The terrain varies from broad open 30 degree slopes to steep narrow chutes on the northeast side of the peak. Probably best done as a day trip beginning from the trailhead, McLoughlin does have enough terrain for two days of skiing if the time and weather permit.

Begin by following the Mt. McLoughlin Trail # 3716. The trail winds through the lower treed slopes and climbs gradually to the west. After about a mile, the trail intersects the Pacific Crest Trail (PCT) near 6,100 feet and by 6,600 feet begins to climb more steeply. The trail is difficult to follow when snow covered and may require a map and compass. Essentially, the trail climbs to the west until it breaks from treeline and then follows the east ridge to the summit. As of 1997 the trail was well flagged with surveyor's tape. Once near treeline (about 8,000 feet), follow the east ridge (to climber's right) that heads west toward the summit. The ridge drops sharply off to the north (climber's right) and gives views into the steeper north facing terrain that is also accessible from the summit. The upper 1,000 to 1,500 feet continues along this ridge to the summit.

The steeper north facing terrain is close to 40 degrees in places and offers nearly 1,500 vertical feet of turns. The drawback to skiing the north facing bowls is the long traverse southward back to the main approach trail or the climb back to the main ridge.

The more southwest facing bowls allow a very clean descent and easy return to the access trail. Several good southwest bowls leading from the summit to treeline. Pick a good line and be sure to keep an eye on the area near treeline where the ridge was accessed. Depending on the snowpack a traverse with or without skis may be necessary to link up good skiable pitches but any time before late May should offer great coverage.

Regardless of descent route, McLoughlin holds classic avalanche prone slopes and all terrain should be evaluated, particularly midwinter.

Looking down McLoughlin's Southeast Side. May

Spring turns on Mt. McLoughlin. May

PART THREE - SOUTHERN OREGON

MT SHASTA – WEST FACE

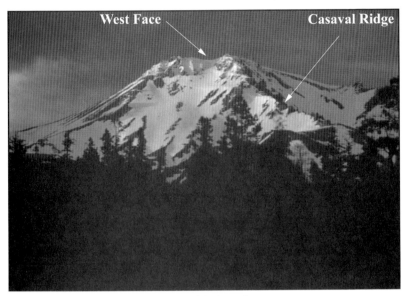

Mt. Shasta's West Face and Casaval Ridge. June

Route Information

- **Season** – April through July
- **Difficulty** - Advanced
- **Total Skiing Vertical** – 5,000 + ft.
- **Starting Elevation** – 6,900 ft.
- **Summit or Goal** – 14,162 ft.
- **Length** – 2 days from Bunny Flat
- **Hazards** – High avalanche potential, elevation

Getting There

- **Access** – From Shasta City, head east on Lake Street, veer left onto the Everitt Memorial Highway as Lake street ends and follow 10.8 miles to the Bunny Flat Trailhead parking area.

MT. SHASTA - WEST FACE

- **Trailhead** – Bunny Flat Trail
- **Map/Information** – USGS Mt. Shasta or Mt. Shasta Wilderness by Tom Harrison Cartography, Mt. Shasta Ranger District - 916-926-4511

At 14,162 feet Mt. Shasta is the second highest of the Cascade volcanos. Few mountains offer over 5,000 vertical feet of skiing but early spring descents on Shasta often feature near 7,000 vertical feet! The mountain has a wide range of skiing and climbing options, some technical and some of moderate difficulty. The West Face of Mt. Shasta is one of the premier ski descents on the mountain. A challenging, yet not very technical ascent of Casaval Ridge combined with the West Face descent make this one of the best advanced ski descents in the Cascades. Located just west of Misery Hill, the West Face runs from 10,000 to 13,200 feet. About a thousand feet beyond the West Face lies Misery Hill and the summit. Although the West Face is close to 1,000 vertical feet short of the summit, it is one of the more sustained steep pitches on Shasta and is easily combined with a descent from the summit area. Although the final 100-200 feet of Shasta is rock, skiing is possible from the saddle above Misery Hill at near 14,000 feet.

Mt. Shasta is one of several Cascade destinations charging for climbing access. As part of the Recreation Fee Demonstration Program legislation passed by Congress in 1996, the Forest Service charges $15.00 per person to climb above 10,000 feet. The permits are valid for three days from the time of issue and are available from the Ranger Station in Shasta City (Monday through Friday 9am-4pm), from a few local merchants or via a self-service box at the trailhead.

Access begins at the Bunny Flat trailhead near 6,000 feet. The most commonly traveled ascent route goes up the Avalanche Gulch drainage. The Avalanche Gulch route is a straightforward, nontechnical, nonglacier climb. A better alternative and the route recommended here is Casaval Ridge. Casaval Ridge is longer than the Avalanche Gulch route and may, depending on snowpack and exact route, require roped travel along exposed sections of the ridge. The Casaval Ridge route, however, is less traveled than the Avalanche Gulch, offers great camping near 10,000 feet and ascends directly along the West Face ski route, allowing evaluation of the descent during your ascent. Climbing Casaval Ridge also allows the majority of your gear to be left at camp during summit day. Casaval Ridge adds variety and challenge to what can otherwise be a long slog up Avalanche Gulch.

Regardless of the route you chosen, begin climbing at the Bunny Flat Trailhead. The route follows a well traveled path to the Horse Camp and the Sierra Club Hut. The Sierra Club Hut serves primarily as a caretaker cabin for the camping in and around the hut area. Drinking water is available when the hut area is snow free and well maintained composting toilets are available near the hut.

The Casaval Ridge route heads north from the hut and ascends the ridge directly behind the hut and west of Avalanche Gulch. A climber's trail quickly gains the ridge and follows up the first drainage you encounter. From the top of the drainage (9,000 feet), traverse left and then continue north in order to gain the ridge on the north side of the drainage. This is Casaval Ridge. The ridge offers great camping near 10,000 - 10,300 feet and camping near 10,000 feet sets up a one day summit attempt from camp. A variety of options from this point allow you to cater the climb to your ability and preferences. The route essentially follows the rock pinnacles of Casaval Ridge up along climber's right of the West Face. Some climbers choose to weave through the rock pinnacles on Casaval while others ascend along climbers left, requiring a steep exposed traverse. Crampons and an ice axe are a necessity, while a rope is at your own discretion. A more moderate route along the base of Casaval Ridge (west side) is also possible. Snow conditions and your ability will dictate your route. Once above the West Face (13,200 feet), the route traverses eastward to climb the appropriately named Misery Hill and then crosses the summit plateau to the final rock pinnacle.

From the summit, ski the summit plateau and Misery Hill if conditions permit. Head west at the base of Misery Hill in order to meet the West Face. The first few turns are in the 40 degree range, but then the slope moderates a bit and holds a consistent pitch for the remainder of the ski to camp near 10,000 feet. Be sure to stay left on the descent in order to regain Casaval Ridge. From camp, descend along the route of ascent.

Another option is to camp in the vicinity of the Sierra Club Hut and make a summit attempt from the hut. Camping at the hut allows climbing either Casaval Ridge or Avalanche Gulch and a descent of the West Face without having to carry all of overnight gear to the summit, but make for a long day.

The Avalanche Gulch route heads northeast from the Sierra Club Hut and simply follows the Climber's Gully (the western most gully descending from Avalanche Gulch) up to Lake Helen. The route climbs steeply above Avalanche Gulch gaining the summit via Red Banks and Misery Hill. Descend the same route or via the West Face.

Descending the lower West Face. June

PART THREE - SOUTHERN OREGON

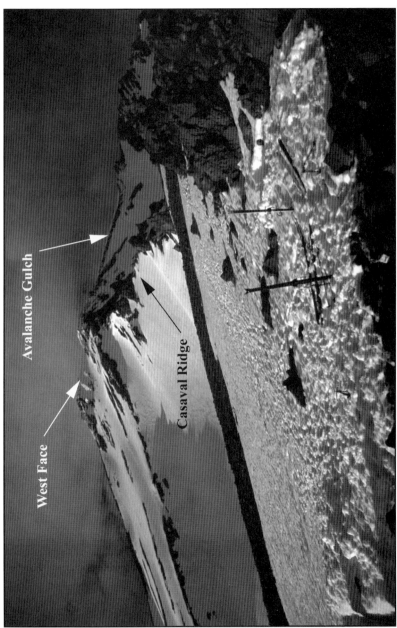

Looking up Casaval Ridge from camp at 10,000 feet. June

PART FOUR
SOUTHERN WASHINGTON

Southern Washington State completes the Southern Cascade region. North of Mt. Adams and Goat Rocks Wilderness, the Cascades take on a new scale. The routes in the Southern Washington region include the classic Mt. St. Helens descents, the larger, yet, nontechnical Mt. Adams and the surprisingly complex Goat Rocks Wilderness. The Southern Washington region generally has weather and snowfall similar to that in the Mt. Hood area, although, be sure to check because weather can vary from region to region.

Mt. St. Helens, although heavily visited, is a classic and technically easy ascent and descent, a must for any Northwest skier. Winter months will see very few visitors, while a beautiful spring weekend may see upwards of several hundred folks making the pilgrimage to the crater rim. Either way, St. Helens is a great introduction to Cascade descents and a classic trip worthy of multiple visits.

Mt. Adams is a massive mountain and, although the size and access length may appear intimidating, Adams allows the intermediate skier a big mountain experience with little technical climbing challenge. The unique location of Goat Rocks between Mt. Adams and Mt. Rainier sets a beautiful stage for a multiple day adventure winter or spring. The terrain in the Goat Rocks area is reasonable for intermediate and better skiers but travel beyond Snowgrass Flats or the White Pass area requires solid backcountry travel and mountaineering skills.

Skiing the Lunch Counter, Mt. Adams. November *Photo: Roger Alfred*

PART FOUR - SOUTHERN WASHINGTON

Goat Rocks Wilderness from the west. September

GOAT ROCKS WILDERNESS SNOWGRASS FLATS

Goat Rocks from above Snowgrass Flats. June

Route Information

- **Season** - December through June
- **Difficulty** - Intermediate to Advanced
- **Total Skiing Vertical** - 2,000 - 3,000+ ft.
- **Starting Elevation** - 3,000 ft. from sno-park / 4,500 ft. from the trailhead
- **Summit or Goal** - Varies
- **Length** - 2 - 3 days, varies with season
- **Hazards** - Moderate avalanche potential

Getting There

- **Access** - From I-5, head east on US 12 for 62 miles. Turn right onto Forest Service Road 21 (Johnson Creek Rd.). Follow Road 21 and signs for Chambers Lake. A sno-park is located at about 7 miles. If conditions permit, continue to left on 2150 to the Snowgrass Flats Trail.

PART FOUR - SOUTHERN WASHINGTON

- ♦ **Trailhead** - Snowgrass Flats Trail # 96
- ♦ **Map/Information** - Green Trails # 302, 303, 334, 335 or USFS Goat Rocks Wilderness, Packwood Ranger District 360-494-5515

Goat Rocks Wilderness is a unique alpine setting located between Mt. Rainier and Mt. Adams in southwestern Washington. Goat Rocks offers an alpine landscape with countless skiing options and ski mountaineering opportunities. The alpine bowls found at Goat Rocks are truly unique to the area and offer extraordinary views of Mt. Rainier and Mt. Adams. A spring venture to Goat Rocks is straightforward, while a winter trip is a committing adventure requiring solid mountain skills. The terrain in the Goat Rocks area does not offer the big vertical ski runs characteristic of many Cascade volcanos but the setting is beautiful and the terrain varied. Moderate bowls fill the area while more demanding terrain can be found by setting off beyond the bowls above Snowgrass Flats. Longer trips to Mt. Curtis Gilbert or a multiple day tour to White Pass can be launched from the Snowgrass Flats area.

Winter and early spring trips require negotiating nearly seven miles of access which may include the snow covered sections of Forest Service Road # 2150. The sno-park is located three miles from the actual Snowgrass Flats Trailhead. Whether skiing or driving Road # 2150, continue to Snowgrass Flats Trail # 96.

The trail ascends gradually until it reaches Goat Creek (approximately 4,200 feet). From the creek, the trail switchbacks up the ridge across from the creek. Beyond the creek, the trail is easily lost if snow covered. After crossing Goat Creek, traverse right (east) until an unnamed creek is reached and then climb beside the creek to Snowgrass Flats. This approach is steeper but the creek makes finding your way easier. A map and compass are essential for the approach when the trail is snow covered.

Snowgrass Flats offers a protected base camp from which to ski and climb. Camping in the flats is prohibited to reduce environmental impact but many options exist near timberline or, during good weather, above the flats. The west facing bowls above Snowgrass Flats provide excellent intermediate to advanced ski terrain. A couple of days are easily spent tracking the bowls above the flats. The area is prone to weather changes and remote in case of emergency so caution is advised for any travel in the area. For more adventure try the east facing slopes of the McCall basin or summit Mt. Curtis Gilbert southwest of Snowgrass Flats (glacier travel required). Exit via Trail # 96 to return. For the experienced backcountry traveler, a multi-day trip can be created by combining this route with the White Pass Route.

Intermediate terrain in Snowgrass Flats, Mt. Rainier in distance. June

WHITE PASS - HOGBACK MT.

Hogback Mt. on the right, as seen from the north. April

Route Information

- **Season** - December through May
- **Difficulty** - Intermediate to Advanced
- **Total Skiing Vertical** - 1,500 ft.
- **Starting Elevation** - 4,500 ft.
- **Summit or Goal** - Hogback Mt., 6,700 ft.
- **Length** - 1 Day or start of multiple day tour
- **Hazards** - Moderate to high avalanche potential on upper east side

Getting There

- **Access** - From I-5, drive east on Route 12 for 84 miles to the White Pass Ski Area. Park at the area and begin from the base of the main lift area.
- **Trailhead** - White Pass Ski Area

WHITE PASS - HOGBACK MT.

◆ **Map/Information** - Green Trails # 302, 303, 334, 335, USFS Goat Rocks Wilderness, Packwood Ranger District - 360-494-5515

Along with stunning views of Mt. Rainier, White Pass offers access to a wide range of backcountry terrain in winter and spring. The approach is made easy in winter by riding the main lift at the White Pass Ski Area to 6,000 feet and beginning a tour from the top of the chair. White Pass offers a one ride ticket for ten dollars. If you are a purist, broke or the area is closed, skin or hike the area by following the cat track up the left flank of the lift area to the top of the main quad lift.

The main destination is Hogback Mt. located almost due south of the ski area's upper chair. Beginning from the upper chair, drop southward to the treed saddle leading away from the area. From the saddle (about 5,800 feet), continue southwest along the ridge. Stays between 5,700 and 5,900 feet until it begins to climb toward a large rock massive separating two drainages. It is best to stay at or near the crest of the ridge until you near the rock. Hogback Mt. lies to the right (southwest) of the rock and is best accessed by staying to the right and below the rock massif. Once treeline is reached, the different ski options become apparent.

Hogback Mt. has moderate terrain on the north and northwest sides while the more east facing bowl wrapping to the left holds advanced terrain. Be wary of the east facing bowl. These slopes are prone to leeward side snow buildup and the ridge commonly holds a cornice much of the season. Many safer northerly and lower angle easterly slopes are also accessible. To exit, follow your route of ascent along the ridge back to the ski area or skirt the left side and connect with the ski area lower and exit near Chair Four.

The area has an abundance of good camping spots below the north facing ridge and is great spot to test your winter camping skills without facing a long approach. The White Pass area also makes for a great launching point for an extended tour into Goat Rocks Wilderness.

PART FOUR - SOUTHERN WASHINGTON

Goat Rocks from summit of Hogback, Mt. Rainier sits off to the right. April

MT. ADAMS - SOUTH SIDE

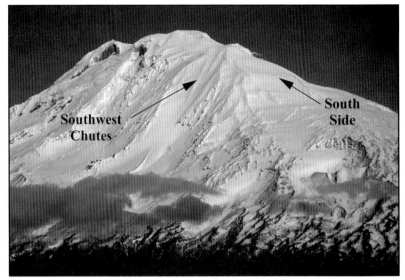

Mt. Adams from the southwest. September

Route Information

- **Season** - March through July
- **Difficulty** - Intermediate to Advanced
- **Total Skiing Vertical** - 5,000 ft. plus, varies by season
- **Starting Elevation** - 5,600 ft. from trailhead
- **Summit or Goal** - 12,276 ft.
- **Length** - 1 - 2 days
- **Hazards** - Low avalanche potential, elevation

Getting There

- **Access** - From State Route 14, drive north on Route 141 to Troutlake. In Troutlake, split right on Road 17, following signs for Mt. Adams Recreation Area. Drive 3 miles and turn left on Road 80. Follow signs for South

Side Climbing Route. Continue 3 miles to Road 8040, turn right and continue as far as conditions permit.
- **Trailhead** - South Climb Trail # 183
- **Map/Information** - Green Trails Mt. Adams West # 366, US Forest Service Mt. Adams Wilderness. Mt. Adams Ranger District, Troutlake, WA - 360-395-2501

The South Side route on Mt. Adams offers the intermediate skier a big mountain experience. Essentially a 'walk up', the South Side requires no technical climbing expertise, aside from self arrest skills, but offers over five thousand vertical feet of skiing. Although Adams can be skied from the summit, the best skiing is from the false summit (about 1,000 vertical feet below and south of the true summit). The true summit is often wind blown and less than enjoyable to ski even in late spring, while the false summit is steeper, longer and corns up more commonly. Early season trips and anyone with hopes of reaching the summit should bring crampons for this route.

The climb follows the South Side Climber's Trail from the upper parking area on Road 8040. Follow the trail through forested terrain climbing moderately for a couple miles to timberline. Near timberline, the trail crosses the upper reaches of the Morrison Creek drainage and begins to climb more steeply. Most of the lower timberline area trail is a wide well travelled route. As elevation is gained to timberline, the trail is less defined and will most likely be snow covered (if it was not at lower elevation). Once above timberline, the most direct approach is to follow the large ridge to your right (northeast). This is Suksdorf Ridge and it can be followed to the broad bench near 9,400 feet. Commonly referred to as the 'Lunch Counter', this bench sits at the base of the pitch leading to the false summit and is a popular area to camp. Continue up to the false summit. The true summit lies across the ridge about a thousand vertical feet away.

The false summit is the highlight of the ski descent. Just over two thousand vertical feet in length, the pitch is a consistent thirty degrees. Skiers left tends to be more moderate, while skiers right holds the pitch more consistently. The remainder of the descent varies. Obvious descent lines follow the ascent route offering wide, gentle terrain. Alternative lines will lead to short, steep pitches and small bowls that are located on the southern aspects of the mountain. In fact, the Crescent Glacier bowls (between 8,600 and 7,400 feet) are a good destination in their own right. Often offering superior conditions when higher elevations are windblown or icy, the Crescent Glacier bowls are a great place to make a winter or early spring trip when snow covered roads create a long access (See 'Crescent Glacier Bowls Route' for more information.)

A second option from the false summit is to ski the Southwest Chutes. Located just west of the ascent route but east of the Avalanche Glacier, the Southwest Chutes are easily seen during the approach along climber's left. The Chutes offer a steeper, narrower line than skiing the face of the false summit. The Southwest Chutes are one of the more sustained, steep descents in the Southern Cascades. The Chutes should only be skied during stable snow conditions and require traversing eastward to rejoin the original ascent route.

MT. ADAMS CRESCENT GLACIER BOWLS

Upper Crescent Glacier Bowl. November   *Photo: Roger Alfred*

Route Information
- **Season** - December through July
- **Difficulty** - Intermediate + to Advanced
- **Total Skiing Vertical** - 1,000 ft. in bowls, plus access
- **Starting Elevation** - 3,400 ft. Wicky Creek Shelter, 5,600 ft. sno-park
- **Summit or Goal** - 8,600 ft.
- **Length** - 2 + days
- **Hazards** - High avalanche potential at the bowls

Getting There
- **Access** - Same as Mt. Adams South Side but in winter and early spring the access Road 8040 will most likely be snow covered somewhere near 3,000 feet. The Wicky Creek Shelter makes a great starting camp if car travel to about 3,400 feet is possible. If not, a long (nearly ten

miles) approach ski/hike is necessary.
- **Trailhead -** South Climb Trail # 183
- **Map/Information -** Green Trails Mt. Adams West # 366, US Forest Service Mt. Adams Wilderness, Mt. Adams Ranger District, Troutlake, WA - 360-395-2501

A great destination when the thought of reaching the summit is daunted by long access or poor snow conditions, the Crescent Glacier is a worthy destination in its own right. The Crescent Glacier Bowls are often unaffected by winds that can scour upper slopes and offer a reasonable winter destination. The winter catch is a long approach may be required. Since an eight plus mile ski on the access road is necessary, be prepared for a two to three day trip in the winter. Alternatively, this area can be skied in the spring and early summer as an alternative to the long trek to the summit. At a minimum, the bowls offer a 1,000 vertical feet of skiing and enough terrain for several laps not to mention the vertical back to where you are parked. The approach is the same as for the South Side Route so be sure to read the description for the South Side.

The bowls are located between 7,400 and 8,600 feet just below the broad slopes leading to the 'Lunch Counter' near 9,400 feet. The area is just southwest of Suksdorf Ridge and is recognized by a small caldera at the base of the glacier.

Even though the Crescent is a glacier, crevasses are not a serious concern. The glacier is located just west of the main south side climb which follows Suskdorf's Ridge. The upper reaches of the glacier have steep (40 plus degree) terrain gradually dropping to gentler more open areas. A variety of camping options exist at timberline or just below the bowls. Always evaluate avalanche hazard prior to skiing the area. The steep upper areas are prime locations for avalanches to release in a variety of conditions.

MT. ST. HELENS PERMIT INFORMATION

Following the 1980 eruption, Mt. St. Helens has become a very accessible and classic Northwest ski descent. The elimination of the upper 1,300 feet created an expansive of moderate terrain that holds snow well into the spring season.

Far from a wilderness experience during the prime spring season, this area regularly sees upwards of a hundred climbers on a clear weekend day. To help manage the activity on Mt. St. Helens and fund federal employees, climbing permits at a cost of $15 per person are required year round. Permits are available on a reservation only basis from May 16th through October 31st. However, from November 1st to May 15th, an unlimited number of permits are issued through Jack's Restaurant and Store located on Route 503, 22 miles east of the I-5 Woodland, WA exit. Jack's opens at 5 am daily.

Before May 16th and after October 31st you simply pay $15 at Jacks; while the controlled permit season from May 16th to October 31st requires a reserved permit and the $15 fee. The controlled permit season allows a total of one hundred permits for any given day. Seventy permits are issued in advance and an additional 30 are available on a first come first serve basis each day. Advance permits are available from Monument Headquarters (Amboy, WA) in person or by mail (Mt. St. Helens National Volcanic Monument Headquarters, Rt. 1, Box 369, Amboy, WA 98601, 360-247-5473). Onsite permits are issued through Jack's on a first come first serve basis the day before you wish to climb. In addition, regardless of the season, all climbers are required to sign in before departing and upon return. Sign-in is also at Jack's.

Much of the prime ski season occurs in March, April and May when reserved permits are not required. However, plenty of good snow can be found in May and June if an advanced permit is obtained. Onsite permits are also an option but there is obviously no guarantee one will be received. Plan ahead or go before May 16th. The last weekend before reserved permit season begins coincides with Mother's Day and is typically a popular weekend to climb and ski down. The act of skiing down Mt. St. Helens in a dress on Mother's Day has been somewhat of a tradition for many free heel skiers over the years. Go for the show or better yet bring a dress and help continue the tradition.

St. Helens offers three different routes for descent: Climber's Bivy/Monitor Ridge, Marble Mountain/Worm Flows and Butte Camp Route. Each route has its own personality and function. Climber's Bivy has the highest starting point (when the road is clear). Marble Mountain offers the best winter access. The Butte Camp Route is probably the least travelled and offers a good option on popular weekends. All routes gain the summit within walking distance of the other routes and all offer at least 4,000 - 5,000 vertical feet of skiing depending on the season. Weather and road conditions will often make the route decision for you, regardless, the skiing is great and St. Helens is a classic Northwest route.

Skiing in dresses, a Mother's Day Tradition. May

MT. ST. HELENS
CLIMBER'S BIVY / MONITOR RIDGE

Monitor Ridge from near treeline. June

Route Information

- **Season** - April through June
- **Difficulty** - Intermediate to Advanced
- **Total Skiing Vertical** - 4,000 + ft.
- **Starting Elevation** - 3,800 ft. if road # 830 is open
- **Summit or Goal** - 8,300 ft.
- **Length** - 1 Day
- **Hazards** - Moderate avalanche potential in gullies and steeper terrain

Getting There

- **Access** - From Woodland, WA, follow Route 503 for 22 miles east to the climber registry at Jack's Restaurant and Store. From Jack's, follow Route 90 east to Cougar, WA and drive another 6.5 miles to Route 83. Turn left on 83 and follow signs for Climber's Bivy. From 83,

drive almost 3 miles, turn left on Road 81 and proceed about 2 miles to Road 830 on your right. Continue up 830 as far as conditions permit.
- **Trailhead** - Climber's Bivy trail # 216A
- **Map/Information-** Green Trails # 364S, USGS Mount St. Helens National Volcanic Monument (NVM), Mt. St. Helens NVM - 360-247-5473

Thanks to the 1980 eruption, Mt. St. Helens is a skier friendly mountain. The absence of glaciers makes St. Helens a nontechnical climb well suited to ski descents. The broad south flanks are an intermediate skier's paradise while the many drainages and ridges offer a mix of terrain to keep advanced skiers entertained. Although technically easy, the climb gains close to 5,000 vertical feet (more if the road is snow covered) and requires a good level of aerobic fitness. The Climber's Bivy Route is the most popular late spring and summer route on the mountain. A clear spring day before permit season has the potential to attract many folks. Do not be surprised to see fifty people on the summit while many more work their way up. Despite the crowds, St. Helens offers great ski terrain. The broad treeless slopes are a Northwest classic.

In an average snow year expect the final access Road 830 to remain snow covered through Memorial Day weekend. Whether the road is driven or hiked, follow it to reach the start of the Climbers Trail # 216A (3,800 feet). The trail heads north about 2 miles through the trees until it meets Monitor Ridge near timberline (4,800 feet). From timberline, gain Monitor Ridge and climb on towards the summit. The route is well traveled and well marked with large wooden posts. Just above timberline is a popular area to camp if you plan on spending the night.

Many descent options exist. A standard route is to follow the route of ascent and is the often the safest, but many options exist on a clear day. Both skier's right and skier's left yield a variety of small drainage and mixed terrain that can be explored. This takes you off the beaten path of the trade route ascent. Beware, it is easy to ski down into a drainage other than the one you ascended, and can leave you far from your car. The alternative drainages can also be used to descend closer to your vehicle if the road is snow covered and the vehicle is parked below the trailhead. All of the drainages immediately west of Monitor Ridge will take you down below the trailhead allowing you to cut out part of the road descent. Be prepared to use a map and compass if this is attempted. Any winter or early season trips warrant taking crampons to aid in climbing hardpack or icy slopes.

5,000 vertical feet of turns. May

MT. ST. HELENS
MARBLE MT. / WORM FLOWS

The Worm Flows from treeline. January

Route Information

- **Season** - December through June
- **Difficulty** - Intermediate to Advanced
- **Total Skiing Vertical** - 5,000 ft.
- **Starting Elevation** - 3,000 ft.
- **Summit or Goal** - 8,300 ft.
- **Length** - 1 day spring, 1-2 days in winter
- **Hazards** - Moderate avalanche potential in gullies and isolated steep terrain

Getting There

- **Access** - From Woodland, WA follow Route 503 east for 22 miles to the climber registry at Jack's Restaurant and Store. From Jack's, follow route 90 east to Cougar, WA and drive another 6.5 miles to Route 83. Turn left

on 83, follow 83 about 6 miles to the Marble Mountain Sno-Park. (The road is closed just beyond the sno-park in the winter.) The sno-park is often closed after April 30th but parking is available in a pullout across from the sno-park entrance Be certain to park completely off the road to avoid ticketing or towing.
- **Trailhead** - Swift Creek Trail # 244
- **Map/Information** - Green Trails # 364 S, USFS Mount St. Helens National Volcanic Monument. Monument HQ - 360-247-5473

Marble Mountain Sno-park offers the best winter access to Mt. St. Helens. It is also the best bet when Road 830 to Climber's Bivy is still fully snow covered. Although the base of Road 830 and the Marble Mountain lot are both at 3,000 feet, something can be said for beginning to hike on a trail versus a snow covered road. When 5,300 vertical feet must be climbed, every edge helps. Marble Mountain is, however, popular with snowmobilers and the lot is often full of them. Do not worry though, the trails are well separated and snowmobiles are rarely encountered beyond the trailhead.

The Swift Creek trail leaves from the northwest side of the lot and quickly moves off into the trees. The trail offers several forks while still in timberline. All forks return to the main trail but the right hand forks are often easier to follow. Should you run into any difficulty simply follow the Swift Creek drainage north and up. Once above timberline, the trail follows along the drainage paralleling the Worm Flows ridge line on climber's right (east). Major erosion in the Swift Creek drainage has occurred in recent years near timberline. Use caution in crossing the drainage and stay on the east side of the drainage until timberline is reached. Similar to Climber's Bivy, good camping options exist around timberline. From timberline, several routes to the summit may be taken. Choose one of the obvious ridgelines leading to the summit or, on a busy day, follow the well worn steps.

Once on the summit, skier's left offers a large open pitch that narrows and divides into several smaller gullies allowing for a variety of descent options. Unlike Climber's Bivy where the descent route is flexible, returning to Swift Creek drainage as you near timberline is necessary to avoid a hike back to your vehicle. Although the upper reaches of St. Helens are often windblown in winter months, the mountain is a great winter descent and can yield great snow at lower elevations when the conditions are right. Due to the short winter days, a two day trip allows for a more relaxed pace.

Spring corn on St. Helens. May

MT. ST. HELENS
BUTTE CAMP ROUTE

First snow on St. Helens, Butte Camp route follows up the left side. September

Route Information

- **Season** - May through June
- **Difficulty** - Intermediate to Advanced
- **Total Skiing Vertical** - 5,000 ft.
- **Starting Elevation** - 3,100 ft.
- **Summit or Goal** - 8,300 ft.
- **Length** - 1 Day, good 2 day trip
- **Hazards** - Moderate avalanche potential in gullies and isolated steep terrain

Getting There

- **Access** - From Woodland, WA follow Route 503 for 22 miles east to the climber registry at Jack's Restaurant and Store. From Jack's, follow Route 90 east to Cougar, WA and drive another 6.5 miles to Route 83. Turn left on 83 and follow 83 for almost 3 miles to the turn off

MT. ST. HELENS - BUTTE CAMP ROUTE

for Road 81 following signs for Climber's Bivy. Continue past the turn off for Road 830 (Climber's Bivy) about two miles looking for the Trailhead (#238) on your right. There is a small parking area at the trailhead. Road 81 is often washed out and badly damaged in the spring. Call for current road conditions.

- **Trailhead** - Blue lake Trail #238 & Butte Camp Trail # 238A
- **Map/Information** - Green Trails # 364S, USFS Mount St. Helens National Volcanic Monument. Monument HQ - 360-247-5473.

The Butte Camp Route is probably the least traveled route option on Mt. St. Helens. This is for a variety of reasons: the starting elevation is 700 vertical feet below Climber's Bivy. At 3.4 miles, access to timberline is the longest of the three routes. The access Road 81 is often impassable due to washouts or is snow covered when the other access roads are clear. However, do not be discouraged. The Butte Camp route offers some of the best timberline camping options and is likely to be less crowded than Climber's Bivy on popular weekends.

The access trail is flat for the first mile until it meets Trail 238A (the actual Butte Camp Trail). From the junction, the trail climbs steadily toward Butte Camp Dome and then steeply to gain the ridge (4,600 feet) just northeast of the actual butte. From the ridge, timberline is quickly reached. Follow the ridge of choice to the summit.

The descent on this route does not offer as many gullies and varieties in terrain as the other routes but does offer several thousand vertical feet of uninterrupted descent. Be sure not to stray too far from the route of ascent once near timberline. From timberline, the best route out is the same as the route in.

PART FOUR - SOUTHERN WASHINGTON

St. Helens crater rim. January

APPENDIX
Avalanche and Weather Resources

Avalanche Information Sources

- **Web Sites**

  The Cyberspace Snow and Avalanche Center
  www.csac.org - Offers a wide range of bulletins, educational information and opportunities and connections to other snow and avalanche related sites.

  The Northwest Avalanche Center
  www.nwn.noaa.gov/sites/nwac - Offers full avalanche bulletins and mountain weather reports
  for Washington and Oregon.

  Westwide Avalanche Network
  www.avalanch.org - Offers many snow and avalanche related sites including reports, photographs and weather resources.

- **Telephone Numbers**

  Oregon Avalanche Report for Mt. Hood and Southern Cascades. **503-326-2400**

  Washington Avalanche Report for Northern Cascades and Olympics. **206-526-6677**

155

APPENDIX

Weather Information Sources

- ### Web Sites

    National Oceanic and Atmospheric Administration
    www.nnic.noaa.gov/NIC/nwsfo.html - Offers all of the NOAA resources and links including National Weather Service links.

    National Weather Service
    www.nws.noaa.gov - Access to National Weather Service sites nationwide.

    The Northwest Avalanche Center
    www.seawfo.noaa.gov/data/forecasts/00latest.sabnw
    The most detailed weather synopsis available for the Cascade mountain region.

    University of Washington Department of Atmospheric Sciences
    www.atmos.washington.edu - Offers detailed satellite and front maps for the Pacific Northwest as well as additional Northwest weather links.

- ### Telephone Numbers

    #### Ski Resort Snow Reports
Crystal Mt.	206-634-3771
Hoodoo	541-822-3337
Mt. Ashland	503-482-2754
Mt. Bachelor	541-382-7888
Mt. Hood Meadows	503-227-SNOW
Ski Bowl	503-222-BOWL
Timberline	503-222-2211
White Pass	509-672-3100

Recommended Reading

Burgdorfer, R., 1983. ***Backcountry Skiing In Washington's Cascades***, The Mountaineers, Seattle, WA, 232 pages.

Daffern, T., 1992, 2nd Edition. ***Avalanche Safety For Skiers and Climbers***, Cloudcap, Seattle, WA, 192 pages.

Dawson, L., 1997. ***Wild Snow***, American Alpine Club, Golden, CO, 254 pages.

Fesler, D., Fredston, J., 1994. ***Snow Sense***, Alaska Mountain Safety Center, Inc. Anchorage, AK, 115 pages.

Graydon, D., 1992, 5th Edition. ***Mountaineering The Freedom Of The Hills***, The Mountaineers, Seattle, WA, 447 pages.

Renner, J., 1992. ***Northwest Mountain Weather***, The Mountaineers, Seattle, WA, 112 pages.

Thomas, J., 1991. ***Oregon High***, Keep Climbing Press, Portland, OR, 127 pages.

Vielbig, K. 1995, 2nd Edition. ***Cross-Country Ski Routes of Oregon's Cascades***, The Mountaineers, Seattle, WA, 255 pages.

Index

A

Alpine and Glade trails 38–40
Avalanche and Weather Resources 155
Avalanche Awareness 24–28
Avalanche Information Sources 155

B

Ball Butte 98
Barrett Spur 68–70
Broken Top 99-100
Butte Camp Route 151-153

C

Central Oregon 90
    Diamond Peak 113-115
    Mt. Jefferson 91
Circumnavigation 41–44
Climbers Bivy / Monitor Ridge 146
Coe Glacier 72–74
Cooper Spur 75–80
Crater Rock 45–47

D

Diamond Peak
    West Side 113-115

E

Equipment 28–29

F

Forward 10
Freezing level 22

G

Goat Rocks Wilderness
    Snowgrass Flats 133-135

H

Heather Canyon 58–60
How to Use this Guide 13-14

I

Illumination Saddle 48–49
Introduction
    Avalanche Awareness 23-28
    Backcountry Access 15-18
    Cascade Weather And Snow 18
    Seasonal notes 15

L

Ladd Glacier 80–82
Langille Bowls 82–84

M

Marble Mountain / Worm Flows 149-151
Middle Sister
    Prouty Pinnacle / North Ridge 106-107
    Southeast Ridge 103-105
Moon Mountain 102
Mt. Adams
    Crescent Glacier Bowls 142-143
    South Side 139-141
Mt. Hood
    East side 56
        Heather Canyon 58–60
        White River Canyon 60–62
        Wy'east face 62
    General area 31
        Tom, Dick and Harry 32–34
    North Side 66
        Barrett Spur 68–70
        Coe Glacier 72–74

INDEX

Cooper Spur 75–80
Ladd Glacier 80–82
Langille Bowls 82–84
Snow Dome 86
South Side 36
  Alpine and Glade trails 38
  Circumnavigation 48–49
  Crater Rock 48–49
  Illumination Saddle 48–49
  Palmer chair access 36
  Summit ski routes 52
Mt. Jefferson
  Jefferson Park Glacier 91
  Park Butte / Park Ridge 95-96
Mt. McLoughlin 122-124
Mt. Shasta 126-128
  Avalanche Gulch 127-128
  Casaval Ridge 126-128
  West Face 126-128
Mt. St. Helens 144
  Climber's Bivy / Monitor Ridge 146-148
  Marble Mountain / Worm Flows 149-151
  Permit information 144-145

N

North Sister
  Southeast Ridge 108-109

O

Overview map 12

P

Preface 11

R

Recommended Reading 157
Resort telephone numbers 156

S

Snow Dome 86
South Sister
  South Side 110-112
Southern Oregon 117
  Mt. Baily 118-119
  Mt. McLoughlin 122-124
  Mt. Scott 117
  Mt. Shasta 126-28
  Mt. Thielsen 117
Southern Washington 130
  Goat Rocks Wilderness 133-135
  Mt. Adams 139-143
  Mt. St. Helens 144-151
  White Pass 136-137
Summit ski routes 52

T

Three Sisters Wilderness 97
  Broken Top 99-100
  Middle Sister 103-107
  North Sister 108-109
  South Sister 110-112
Tom Dick and Harry Mountain 32–34

W

Weather Information Sources 156
White Pass
  Hogback Mt. 136-137
White River Canyon 60–62
Wy'east face 62

159

. . . . *Peace*